Fabric Silhouettes

QUILTED TREASURES FROM THE FAMILY ALBUM

Louise Handley

C&T PUBLISHING

Text © 2006 Louise Handley

Artwork © 2006 C&T Publishing, Inc.

Publisher: Amy Marson

Editorial Director: Gailen Runge

Acquisitions Editor: Jan Grigsby

Editor: Candie Frankel

Technical Editors: Gayl Gallagher, Georgie Gerl

Copyeditor/Proofreader: Wordfirm, Inc.

Design Director/Cover & Book Designer: Christina D. Jarumay

Illustrator: John Heisch

Production Assistant: Matt Allen

Photography: Luke Mulks and Diane Pedersen unless otherwise noted

Published by C&T Publishing, Inc., P.O. Box 1456, Lafayette, CA 94549

Front cover: *End of the Ride*, *My Little Cowboys*, *Reunion*, and *Trick-or-Treat* by Louise Handley

Back cover: *Barbershop Harmony*, *Birthday Party Fun*, and *'Twas the Night Before Christmas* by Louise Handley

Library of Congress Cataloging-in-Publication Data

Handley, Louise

  Fabric silhouettes : quilted treasures from the family album / Louise Handley.

    p. cm.

  Includes index.

  ISBN-13: 978-1-57120-347-2 (paper trade)

  ISBN-10: 1-57120-347-8 (paper trade)

  1. Appliqué. 2. Quilting. 3. Silhouettes. 4. Fabric pictures. I. Title.

  TT779.H34 2006

  746.46'041--dc22

                    2005033572

Printed in China

10 9 8 7 6 5 4 3 2 1

To all those who desire to create.

ACKNOWLEDGMENTS

My thanks to...

Our wonderful children and grandchildren for inspiring so many great snapshots

My husband, Dick, for his encouragement and tireless typing and retyping of the manuscript

My sister Eleanor for appearing with me in Sisters *and for suggesting the arched overlay*

The kids in Group 9

My students over the years, who have taught me and inspired me to create

And to Sue, for understanding.

CONTENTS

INTRODUCTION

Traditional cast-shadow silhouette

T he striking black-and-white silhouette art of years gone by and my love of creative quiltmaking have been the inspiration behind *Fabric Silhouettes*.

Silhouette artistry can be traced throughout history—examples have even been found on Stone Age cave walls! In the United States before the emergence of photography, itinerant silhouette artists traveled the cities and back roads, delighting their customers by creating recognizable likenesses. These silhouettes were almost always cut in profile and included only the head and shoulders of the subject. Scenery and houses were also popular subjects.

Here Comes the Parade quilt and original photo

Silhouettes are traditionally created in one of two ways. A truly gifted silhouette artist is able to study the person in profile and cut the silhouette freehand without a pattern or drawing. The entire process can take as little as one and a half minutes. In the cast-shadow method, the artist directs a light source past a seated subject in such a way as to cast a profile on a wall or screen. The artist then outlines the profile while the subject sits perfectly still. The drawing that results can be cut out and mounted on contrasting paper, or it can be filled in solidly with paint or ink. A black silhouette on a white or cream background is the classic look for this fascinating art form.

The silhouette designs in my quilting are taken from my own family albums. After careful modification, and often some repositioning, a favorite old snapshot becomes a wall hanging, a quilt, or an art piece suitable for framing. I call them Snapshot Silhouettes, because I go beyond the traditional facial profile to create them. I feel free to use whatever features the snapshot offers me, and I add extra elements when I need them. You will be pleasantly surprised at how accurately a silhouette captures the physical characteristics, and even the body language, of your subject. It is a delight when people are able to recognize the person you have silhouetted!

You may copy the projects in this book for your use in small wall hangings, framed art, or quilts. They can also guide you in creating paper silhouettes for note cards, memory albums, and other paper crafts. But your greatest thrill will come from trying my simple techniques with your own photos to create one-of-a-kind silhouettes.

The Snapshot
SILHOUETTE

The Right Photo

As you page through your family photo album or rummage through that shoe box stuffed with snapshots, look first for figures that do not overlap. Keep in mind that your subject does not have to be in profile. The best pictures will show the person doing something—riding a bike, flying a kite, walking, skiing, or gardening. Choose several photos, in case your first choice doesn't work out.

When you find a photo you like, squint or remove your glasses to blur the background. If you were to draw only an outline of the subject, would the arms, legs, and head be visible? Would the activity be recognizable? Techniques you can employ to transform even a poor photo into an interesting silhouette include moving an arm or a leg, creating background space between subjects, or adding a tool, hat, or other prop.

Do you want more than one person in your Snapshot Silhouette? No problem. The figures don't even have to come from the same picture or be the same size, as the photocopier can easily and quickly reduce or enlarge them. Compare the project illustrations and original photos in this book to get an idea of the transformations that are possible. Don't give up on an image you'd like to use until you've learned all the ways you can modify it.

> **TIP** *If your collection of snapshots doesn't yield any interesting poses, try staging a photo shoot. Snap candid shots when your subject is working, playing, walking, or driving. For a more revealing silhouette, try to capture a profile of the subject's face. After the photos are developed, choose one or two for your silhouette. If you use a digital camera, you can make a selection on your computer screen.*

The Cast-Shadow Method

Use the cast-shadow method to create a formal silhouette. When you are finished, reduce or enlarge your drawing or photograph on a photocopier. Treat the photocopy like any other image in the development of a Snapshot Silhouette.

1. Tape a large piece of white paper to the wall. Seat your subject next to the wall, allowing enough space to reach in and trace.

2. Direct a light source, such as a slide projector or a lamp with a can-type shade and adjustable arm, toward the subject. Adjust the light source to cast a profile shadow onto the paper.

3. Trace the cast shadow with a soft-lead pencil, making short, choppy marks (instead of drawing, you can photograph the shadow *without* a flash).

4. Add a slanted or rounded line at the bottom of the tracing to complete the silhouette at the neck, shoulders, or waist.

Original drawing

Thirteen, 12$\frac{1}{2}$″ × 12$\frac{1}{2}$″, quilted and traditionally framed

Thirteen, 13$\frac{1}{2}$″ × 13$\frac{1}{2}$″

Sizing the Photo

Once you have selected a photo to work with, make a photocopy of it. The copy doesn't have to be photo quality. Even a very blotchy copy will work as long as the outline is visible. Use scissors to cut away the excess background, leaving a 1″ margin around the subject.

Now enlarge or reduce the image to your heart's content. Your purpose here is to try several sizes until you find the size you would like to use for your completed silhouette. A medium or large silhouette (about 7″ to 8″) is better for a beginning project. To make a very large silhouette, cut the photocopy in half or in quarters, enlarge each piece separately, and then tape the pieces together. Don't make it too large, however. Remember that the framing, accent, and binding fabrics will add extra inches to the silhouette background.

If you are working with two or more subjects and they come from separate photos, you may need to resize each image at a different percentage to make them proportional to one another. A rule of thumb is to make the heads proportionally the same. Of course, if you are designing your composition to show depth, the heads in the background would be smaller and the heads in the foreground would be larger.

After you have gained some experience, don't be afraid to try smaller silhouettes in your projects. With the right scissors, a paper-backed fusible web on the fabric, and a little practice, you'll find that even small, intricate silhouettes are quite easy to cut out.

> **TIP** *Photocopier use is charged by the page, even if you are running test images. To economize and keep your costs down, try fitting more than one photo on each page.*

The Tracing

The next step is to trace the outline of the resized image onto tracing paper. Use a sheet of tracing paper that is about 3″ larger all the way around than the silhouette to accommodate corrections or additions later in the process. Tape the image copy to a hard surface, layer the tracing paper over it, and tape down the corners.

If your photocopied images are blurred or blend into the background, go over the outlines with a sharp pencil to make them more visible. Using a lightbox or taping the sheets to a window may make tracing easier.

Use a sharp pencil with a soft lead to trace the outline of the person or figure to be silhouetted. Short, choppy marks will produce a more accurate tracing than long, thin lines, which are hard to draw accurately. Include basic clothing outlines, as well as any object that helps tell what is going on in the picture. Use a ruler to draw all straight lines and a compass for circles. *Make the tracing as accurate as possible.*

Look at your completed tracing with a critical eye. Are you able to identify parts of the body and the activity? If not, you will need to modify your tracing for clarity. Very few snapshots will yield a perfect tracing. Typically, parts of the subject or important identifying objects will be hidden from view or cropped out of the snapshot. Occasionally, you may have to give up on a photo, but don't do that until you've read about the various techniques you can use to enhance your tracing and create a truly exciting Snapshot Silhouette.

FILL IN BLOCKED OR HIDDEN AREAS

Identify parts of the image that are blocked or that extend beyond the view shown in the photo. Draw them onto the tracing.

The tricycle back wheels were completed by tracing around bottle caps. The foot plate was sketched in.

Detail from *Birthday Party Fun* original photo

SUBSTITUTE MISSING PARTS

You don't need to be able to draw very well to fill in missing parts of the body. Select the parts and poses you need from other photos or from clothing advertisements and catalogs. Reduce or enlarge the pictures to fit your silhouette, and trace them in place.

End of the Ride original photo

The missing feet for this tracing came from a second photo.

▧ FRAME THE IMAGE

If missing parts are too difficult or awkward to fill in, try framing the image and screening them out. Lay a picture frame or mat over the tracing to find the opening size and shape that fit. This technique is especially useful for close-ups that cut off the top or sides of the head.

An oval mat preserves the intimacy of the original close-up photo.

▧ ADD SPACES

Using spaces of various sizes is another way to define the outline. Spaces are generally triangular and open up larger areas.

Added spaces lend definition to the skirt, torso, and front wheel in *Birthday Party Fun*.

▧ ADD SLITS AND SLIVERS

Does the image have areas that are just not clear? The biggest problems occur where clothes and body parts come together and overlap. Just a few carefully placed slits and slivers can change a confusing shape into an elegant and refined image. Look carefully at the silhouette examples throughout the book and see if you can pick out the slits and slivers. Now try adding some to your tracing. Draw very narrow slits and slivers that taper to a point at each end. One edge will be the defining edge and must be carefully drawn and cut. The space for the sliver extends from the defining edge. If you don't like the result, gently erase your pencil lines and try again. It is very important not to cut off and isolate any one area; you want to be able to handle the entire silhouette as a single piece when it is cut out. Strive for simplicity.

Original photo

A few slits and slivers define lapels, collar, dress folds, jawlines, and wisps of hair.

Style Notes

Vintage paper silhouettes are difficult to find and expensive to purchase. Because early silhouettes were often made with poor-quality paper, they have long since turned to dust. Painted silhouettes, however, are quite easy to find. In a painted silhouette, the background paper shows through unpainted areas that correspond to the slits, slivers, and spaces in a cut silhouette. Many times the background is black paper, and the artist paints the silhouette with gold paint. Another method is to paint the silhouette on glass and add a backing paper, which shows through the open areas. The background can be an elaborate landscape, dried flowers, tinfoil, or silk fabric.

Silhouettes can also be hollow cut. In this technique, the silhouette is cut out as a single piece. The background paper that remains is mounted over contrasting paper to reveal the silhouette. If the artist is careful, the cutout silhouette can also be used. The result is two silhouettes from one cutting.

The vintage silhouettes shown here are worth studying to get an idea of where to add slits, slivers, and spaces to your Snapshot Silhouettes. Note the subtlety of the art form. Slits and slivers must be very narrow to be realistic.

Pair of silhouettes, technique unknown

Cut silhouette

Silhouette painted in gold on black background

Painted silhouette on domed glass, realistic paper background

◈ SLASH THE TRACING

Slashing lets you separate and expand a tracing. It provides more background in crowded areas so you can better define arms, legs, and other shapes that touch one another. Trim the tracing ¼″ to ½″ beyond the outline. Use scissors to cut into the tracing 1″ or deeper. Spread the edges very slightly, set a scrap of tracing paper underneath, and apply clear tape. Press the tracing flat with your hand, pleating or tucking the paper as needed, and tape to hold.

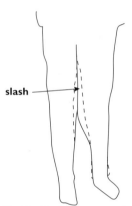

slash

Trick-or-Treat original photo

Slashing the tracing separates the red legs for better definition.

◈ MOVE PART OF THE IMAGE

Moving part of the image works well with arms and legs. Often a bent limb will show off the subject in a more realistic pose than a straight limb will. To bend a limb, trace the forearm or the leg from the knee down on a small piece of tracing paper. Put the new tracing under the big tracing, move it around until you find a position you like, and trace the outline. Be sure to erase any original tracing lines.

My Little Cowboys original photo   Original tracing   Modified tracing

◈ ADD LINE WORK

Fine, narrow details, such as bicycle spokes or blades of grass, are simply too difficult to cut out. Draw them onto your tracing now so that you can ink them onto your background fabric later with a fine-tip permanent pen.

End of the Ride original photo

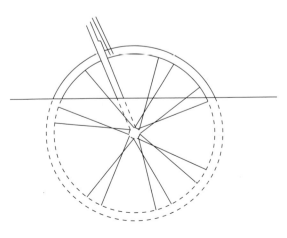

Bicycle spokes are drawn in.

PUNCH TINY OPENINGS

Tiny openings in the silhouette impart a delicate, filigree look that can help you depict floral bouquets, stars, printed clothing, buttons, jewelry, lace, and twinkly lights. Mark these areas for punching on the pattern. Later, you will use a pliers-type punch to create these tiny openings in the bonded fabric. The punched-out pieces can also be used.

Autumn Wedding original photo detail

A bridal bouquet. Mark the tracing
to show where to punch later.

USE A NOVELTY FABRIC

Do some areas of the tracing leave you wishing for something more? Occasionally, you may wish to call attention to a particular area of the silhouette by using a brighter fabric or a novelty print. Printed fabrics include images of flowers, tools, sports equipment, and holiday themes, among many others. If the proportions are right, these images can be bonded, cut out, and used to accent the silhouette or the background. As you work with your tracing, think ahead and dip into your fabric stash for ideas. When you find a print that will work, set it aside and mark an **X** on your tracing to show where it will go.

Welcome Home original photo

An *X* on the tracing is a reminder to
use the special fabric.

A fabric with star motifs for the balloon silhouette

BORROW A DESIGN

Do you want to add someone or something from another picture? How about a hat, ribbon, or kite? Extra images of people, animals, buildings, or accessories can help viewers grasp the theme and setting of your silhouette art more readily.

Lighthouse photo

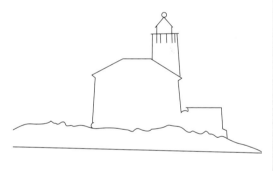

Lighthouse tracing

Modified Tracing Checklist

Have you tried everything to enhance your Snapshot Silhouette? Use this checklist to find out.

☐ **Fill in blocked or hidden areas,** as well as areas beyond the camera's range.

☐ **Substitute missing parts,** such as arms and legs, to make the silhouette complete.

☐ **Frame the image** to camouflage a problem of missing parts.

☐ **Add slits and slivers** to define key lines in the body or clothing.

☐ **Add spaces** to separate and define key areas of the design.

☐ **Slash the tracing** for more separation between parts.

☐ **Move part of the image** to have the subject strike a more interesting pose.

☐ **Add line work or lettering** to ink in later.

☐ **Mark tiny openings** for a lacy appearance, to punch in later.

☐ **Use a novelty fabric** for added emphasis.

☐ **Borrow a design** from somewhere else.

Fabric SELECTION

Selecting fabrics for a silhouette project takes time, but it is also exciting and just plain fun. Bring your photocopy and this book with you when you shop for fabric. You probably won't find the exact prints pictured here, as manufacturers seldom reprint their designs, but you can use my selections as a guide. Picking out your own colors and prints is part of the artistic experience of making a quilt. If you need advice, fabric and quilt store clerks are very happy to help you. You only have to ask.

You will need at least four different fabrics for your project (see the fabric placement diagram). Historically, silhouettes have been black on a white or an off-white background, even though other colors of paper and ink were available. For Snapshot Silhouettes, a softer, less stark contrast is often preferable and easily achievable through a variety of cotton quilting fabrics. Look for background, framing, accent, and binding fabrics that reflect the theme of your project. Color-coordinated fat quarter bundles are always a good choice.

Fabric placement

SILHOUETTE

Pick a dark, high-quality cotton fabric for the silhouette. Black is the traditional choice, but you might also choose a dark color such as brown, maroon, deep green, or navy. The silhouette fabric does not have to be a solid; you can use a mottled print as long as the overall look suggests a solid. The weave should be as tight as you can find; look for a high thread count. To check for a tight weave, hold the fabric up to the light or lay it across a white background and make sure no light or white shows through.

A dark brown silhouette suggests the sepia tones of an old photo.

Mottled navy is less stark than black against this grassy background.

TIP *Avoid prewashing new silhouette fabrics. That crisp manufacturer's finish will help protect your quilted art from damage by light or dust. Make an exception for bed quilts and other pieces that will receive heavy wear.*

BACKGROUND

Choose a background fabric with your photocopy, tracing, and silhouette fabric samples in hand. The background fabric will help set the stage for your silhouette. Look first for a medium to light fabric, for good contrast with the dark silhouette. Focus in on fabrics that are simple, yet interesting. Look for themes and colors that express the story line of your photo. Small, indistinct florals, geometrics, monochromatic patterns, and grasses are all good choices, as long as they are not too busy. Stay away from boring solids or any design with a white background, unless you are trying to reproduce a vintage black-and-white silhouette. In that case, look for a white-on-white fabric to create more interest.

View your samples side by side to find a combination you like. Does the silhouette fabric stand out? Is the background too busy? Will a design in the background fabric compete with the silhouette or enhance it? A simple background with high contrast is your goal.

A blue batik background creates a magical starry evening. Detail from *'Twas the Night Before Christmas.*

A cloud background fabric contributes to this seashore mood. Detail from *Sisters.*

FRAMING

Like a good picture frame, the framing fabric surrounds the silhouette art, completing it and showcasing it in a harmonious way. Look for a theme fabric that relates to your story line for more interest. The framing fabric should have a touch of the dark silhouette color in it, if possible, to help with overall blending. The framing fabric may also be used for the binding.

ACCENT

The accent fabric is a narrow strip placed between the background and the framing. Look for a fabric that picks up a color from the framing fabric. The accent fabric may also be used for the binding.

A red accent strip prevents the background and framing prints from blending together in this patriotic silhouette. The bright color sets off the silhouettes and adds sparkle. Detail from *Here Comes the Parade*.

FABRIC PALETTES

Left to right in each palette: silhouette, background, framing, accent

The Fabric
SILHOUETTE

This chapter describes how to create a fabric silhouette and apply it to the background fabric. First you will apply a paper-backed fusible web (bonding material) to the silhouette fabric. Then you'll transfer the modified tracing to the paper backing using graphite transfer paper and a stylus. This method of transfer provides an accurate cutting line. You then will cut out the silhouette, fuse it to the background fabric, and stitch it in place. A final step is to draw in missing elements with a fine-tip permanent pen.

▥ HANDLE WITH CARE

To prevent wrinkles, creases, and frayed edges, handle the silhouette-in-progress as little as possible and keep it flat at all times. Slide a large piece of cardboard or foam core underneath it to transfer it back and forth between the ironing board and work surface. Should your work be interrupted, store your silhouette-in-progress flat in a large folder or envelope.

You will need:

- **Silhouette and background fabrics** (see page 14).
- **Snapshot Silhouette tracing pattern** (see page 6).
- **Snapshot Silhouette supplies.** These supplies include a transparent 6″ ruler, compass, scissors, tape, and picture frames or mats (see page 5).
- **Lightweight paper-backed fusible web**. I prefer HeatnBond Lite, which can be bought by the yard at most fabric stores. Cut convenient lengths and flatten them under a stack of magazines. Roll the excess for storage.
- **Iron and ironing board.** Protect your ironing board surface with parchment paper or a sheet that has a nonstick coating, as bonding adhesive is very hard to remove.
- **Graphite transfer paper.** Graphite transfer paper is sold at artist supplies stores.
- **Sharp graphite pencil or stylus.**
- **X-Acto knife and extra blades.**
- **Self-healing cutting mat.**
- **Small scissors with sharp blades.**
- **Seam ripper.**
- **Sewing machine.**
- **Sewing machine needles.** Use a sharp quilting needle #75/11 or a jeans needle #90/14.
- **Thread.** Choose 100% cotton thread in a dark color that matches the silhouette fabric.
- **Fine-tip permanent pens.** Fine-tip permanent pens come in various sizes and colors. My favorite brand is the Pigma Micron pen. Start with size 05 for fine lines and size 08 for thicker lines in a color to match your silhouette fabric. For very fine lines, you may wish to add a size 005. The inked lines are permanent, waterproof, and fade proof.
- **Reducing glass or mirror.** A reducing glass or mirror lets you view work in progress as if from a distance. It helps you identify problems of balance and proportion that are difficult to see up close.
- **Mini-iron.** A mini-iron is very helpful when you are applying small parts of the silhouette to the background. Mini-irons are available at most fabric and quilting stores.
- **Long-handled tweezers.** To avoid burning your fingers, use tweezers to position small items for bonding.

APPLYING THE FUSIBLE WEB

> **TIP** *When the fusible instructions say "set iron on silk setting," you'd better believe it! Too hot an iron will cause the bond to release. If this happens to you, allow the fabric to cool and start the bonding process again.*

1. Cut a piece of dark silhouette fabric slightly larger than your traced pattern. Cut a piece of paper-backed fusible web the same size as the fabric.

2. Press the silhouette fabric to remove all wrinkles. Wrinkles that are not pressed out will be bonded in place.

3. Reset the iron to the proper bonding temperature, following the manufacturer's instructions.

4. Lay the silhouette fabric wrong side up on the ironing board. Place the paper-backed fusible web on it, adhesive side down. Press to set the bond, following the manufacturer's instructions. Allow to cool in place. *Do not peel off the paper backing.*

5. Optional: Repeat Steps 1–4 to bond any special fabrics that you have chosen for parts of the design marked with an *X*.

MARKING THE DESIGN

> **TIP** *Pretest the fusible web to make sure the paper backing accepts a graphite transfer. On some brands, the papers are waxy or coated and the transfer will not take, no matter how hard you press with the stylus.*

1. Lay the bonded fabric on a smooth, flat surface with the paper side up.

2. Place the modified tracing *facedown* on top of the papered side of the fusible web. Tape it down in a few places to prevent shifting. Even though the silhouette pattern is turned wrong side up now, the design will appear right side up when the process is complete.

3. Slip a piece of graphite paper, shiny side down, *between* the tracing and the paper-backed fusible web. Secure it with tape so the papers won't slip.

4. Use a sharp pencil or stylus to go over the traced outline and modifications. Work slowly and carefully. Use a small ruler to draw straight lines. Use a compass to draw circles. Omit thin lines that will be inked in later. Also omit outlining parts of the design marked with an *X*, which will be marked on special fabrics (see Step 6).

5. Carefully lift one edge of the tracing and graphite paper and check the transferred image. Add any lines that you missed. Untape the modified tracing and set it aside.

6. Repeat Steps 1–5 to mark the *X* parts of the design on any special silhouette fabrics you prepared.

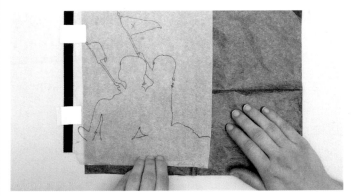

Insert graphite paper.

Go over the design.

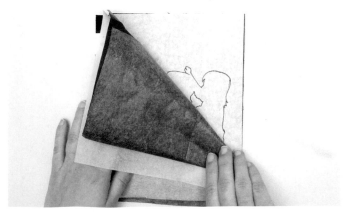

Make sure the transfer comes through.

CUTTING THE SILHOUETTE

TIP *Pick a time when you are fresh and relaxed to cut out your silhouette. It's easy to make mistakes when you are tired.*

1. Use large scissors to trim off the excess bonded fabric ¼″ to ½″ beyond the silhouette outline. Removing the excess will make the detail cutting easier.

2. Cut along the silhouette outline with small, sharp scissors. Hold the scissors with your thumb and middle finger for better control. Hold the silhouette to the left of the scissors blade (reverse if you are left-handed) so that you can see the cutting line better. Use a seam ripper to poke a starter hole for cutting in tight areas.

3. Use a sharp X-Acto knife and a cutting mat to cut narrow slits, slivers, and small triangular areas that you cannot reach or cut comfortably with scissors. Pull the blade toward you for each cut, turning the silhouette as you work. Work slowly and carefully. When the blade becomes dull, sharpen it on a whetstone or insert a new blade. If you should accidentally cut off a necessary area, save the piece (you can bond it to the background separately). *Do not remove the paper backing.*

4. Repeat steps 1–3 to cut out any silhouette shapes marked on special fabrics. If you will be punching holes, test your punch on a scrap of bonded fabric to make sure it is sharp and unclogged. Punch the holes last. Don't forget to clip your "hanging chads."

The rough cut

The detail cut

More detail

CREATING THE LAYOUT

TIP *Use Fray Check to stabilize a corner, point, or edge of the silhouette that starts to ravel. Pick up a bit of Fray Check from the tube with the point of a toothpick or pin and touch it to the cut edge. Avoid getting Fray Check on the flat surface of a dark fabric, as it may sometimes be visible.*

1. Lay the background fabric right side up and press it flat.

2. Reset the iron to the proper bonding temperature, following the manufacturer's instructions.

3. Lay the bonded silhouette on a flat surface, paper side up. Slowly and carefully peal off the paper backing, exposing the adhesive.

4. Place the silhouette, adhesive side down, on the background fabric. Use the tracing pattern to double-check the placement.

5. Press to set the bond, following the manufacturer's instructions. Pay particular attention to corners and small protrusions, to make sure they fuse in place. Bond any special fabric pieces that you prepared for the silhouette. Allow to cool in place.

6. View the bonded silhouette through a reducing glass or in a mirror to see if the design looks balanced and complete. It is not too late to add a person or an item to fill in a bare space.

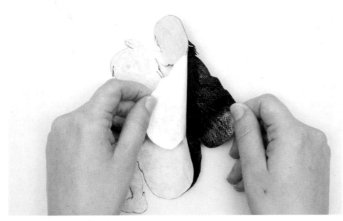

Peel off the paper backing.

Fuse the silhouette to the background.

Use a mini-iron and tweezers in delicate spots.

STITCHING

> **TIP** *If you sew off the edge, or not close enough to it, use a seam ripper and work from the back of the piece to remove the bad stitching. Cut the thread every third or fourth stitch. Then use tweezers to gently pull out the surface threads. Pulling too aggressively will cause the silhouette fabric to fray.*

1. Install a new, sharp quilting needle #75/11 or a jeans needle #90/14 in the sewing machine. Thread the machine with dark cotton thread that matches the silhouette fabric. Set the machine for a straight stitch and a short stitch length, about 15 stitches per inch or a size that looks good on your material.

2. Position the work on the machine bed, with the silhouette to the left of the needle. Starting in an inconspicuous area of the silhouette, stitch slowly and carefully around the outside edge of the silhouette, as close as possible to the edge without slipping off.

3. Stop with the needle in the down position and lift the presser foot to pivot the work. On tight curves and in areas with lots of detail, you may need to do this repositioning every few stitches. Strive for rounded curves and sharp corners. Set the stitch length even tighter for details such as hands, fingers, and toes. Watch the needle and the center guide mark on your machine to ensure accuracy.

4. When the stitching reaches the starting point, clip the threads, pull the top threads through to the underside, and tie them in a knot. You can backtack at the beginning and end of a stitching line instead, if you prefer.

5. Repeat steps 2–4 to stitch around any slivers, slits, or small openings.

6. Change the thread color and repeat Steps 2–5 to stitch any elements in the silhouette that were cut from special or contrasting fabric.

7. Examine the silhouette to see if there are any fuzzy or frayed edges. Carefully fold back the background fabric in these areas, slide the scissors blade between the silhouette and the background, and trim off the excess threads. Practice this technique on a sample silhouette before attempting it on your project. If the raveling is excessive, choose a fabric that is more tightly woven for your next silhouette.

Needle position

Stitches are tight and close to the edge.

Trimming a frayed edge

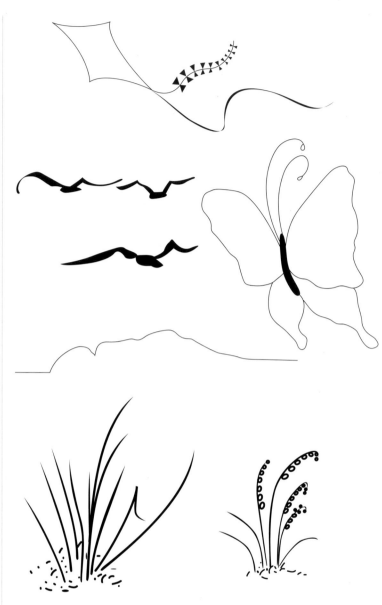

LINE WORK

Look carefully at your design. Are all of the features clear, or is something missing? Does your silhouette appear to be floating? There may be a detail in your original photo, such as a balloon string or a horizon line, that is important to the scene but that you were not able to capture in the silhouette itself. Lettering or simple images also may need more emphasis.

Draw a few lines on your modified tracing to try out your ideas. A horizon line, a few steps, or a clump of grass can anchor a subject that appears to be floating. Use a ruler to draw straight lines. Keep these additions simple, to avoid detracting from the silhouette. Thick-and-thin line work is more effective than thin lines and adds a dimensional effect.

Once you have lines you like, take a deep breath and draw the same lines on your background fabric. Use a fine-tip permanent pen size 05 for fine lines and size 08 for heavy lines. If you are hesitant to work freehand, transfer guidelines to the fabric using the modified tracing and graphite paper. Then ink over the traced lines.

When your silhouette is complete, sign and date your artwork. Artwork? Art? Yes! You are now a silhouette artist, working in textiles.

PAPER CRAFTING

The silhouette techniques described in this chapter are not limited to fabric. Did you know that fusible web also works with paper and cardboard? You can use the techniques taught in this chapter to cut silhouettes from fabric or colored paper and bond them to various backgrounds, including wood! Paper or fabric silhouettes make perfect additions to memory albums, greeting cards, and other paper crafts. Follow the manufacturer's instructions and make test pieces to find the right bonding temperatures for various materials.

Framing AND FINISHING

THE FABRIC FRAME

A fabric frame sets off the simplicity of the silhouette and adds to the overall artistry. Its mitered corners mimic the look of traditional framing. The finished framing strip is typically 2″ to 5″ wide (see Framing Strip Dimensions on page 62) and may or may not have an accent strip.

You will need:

- **Rotary cutter.**
- **Clear rotary cutting ruler.** This ruler should be 6″ × 24″ and have 45° angle markings.

1. Mark corner dots A, B, C, and D on the background fabric ¼″ from each edge. Center a framing strip on the AB edge, right sides together. Make sure that the strip extends evenly beyond the background at each end. Stitch from A to B as shown, making a ¼″ seam allowance and starting and stopping ¼″ from the edge. Press toward the framing strip.

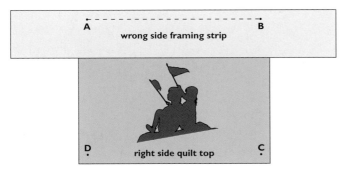

Stitch from A to B.

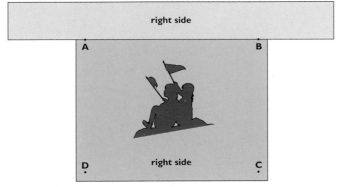

Press.

2. Sew a separate framing strip to each remaining edge in the same way, starting and stopping ¼″ from the edge. Press toward the framing strips. Let the ends overlap and hang loose.

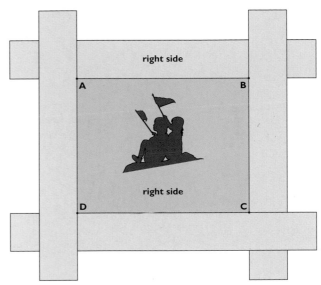

Sew a strip to each edge.

3. Fold the piece diagonally, wrong side out, matching the edges of two adjacent framing strips. Flip the seam allowances toward the background fabric so that the ends of the strips lie flat. Use the 45° line on the rotary cutting ruler to confirm that the angle of the fold line is a true 45° and adjust as needed.

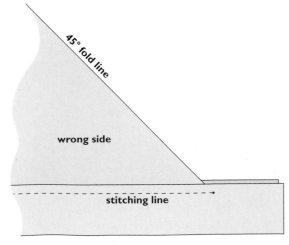

Fold one corner at a 45° angle.

4. Align a ruler on the fold line, letting it extend beyond the framing strips. Run a pencil against the edge of the ruler to draw a 45° stitching line on the top framing strip. Draw a cutting line ¼″ beyond the stitching line. Cut on the cutting line through both layers. Stitch on the stitching line.

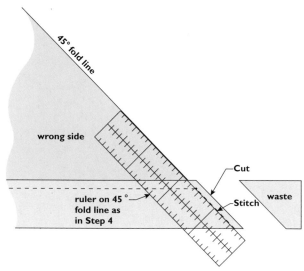

Cut and stitch the miter.

5. Unfold the work. Press open the mitered seam. Trim off the dog-ears. Repeat Steps 3–5 to miter each corner.

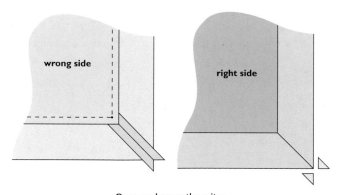

Open and press the miter.

Accent Strips

An accent strip is an optional fabric border that appears between the silhouette background and the fabric frame. You fold and sew the accent strip to the framing strip at the beginning of the assembly process. Both strips are then handled as a single unit for joining and mitering. This construction method helps prevent a wavering stitching line, which is very noticeable in strips narrower than 1½″.

1. Decide on the accent strip's finished width—typically ½″ to 1″. To determine the cut width, multiply the finished width by 2, and add ½″ for the seam allowances. Cut an accent strip to this width for each framing strip.

2. Fold the accent strip in half lengthwise, right side out. Press to set the crease.

3. Place the accent strip on the framing strip, right sides up and raw edges matching. Machine baste ¼″ from the raw edges. You can stitch down the folded edge, or you can leave it loose and stitch it after the quilt top is assembled. Leaving it loose adds dimension to the finished quilt.

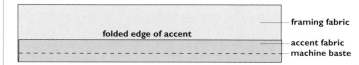

Adding an accent strip

4. Repeat steps 2–3 for each set of strips. Follow Steps 1–5 in The Fabric Frame (page 21) to join the strips to the background and miter the corners. Be sure to place the accent strips on the edge of the fabric frame that attaches to the background.

Layering and Quilting

For the backing, cut a piece of fabric approximately 1″ wider and 1″ longer than the quilt top. Press the backing fabric, lay it right side down on the work surface, and tape it to the surface. Cut a slightly larger piece of lightweight batting, such as Warm & Natural low-loft batting, and lay it on top. Layer the silhouette piece on top, right side up. Smooth the layers and secure them with small safety pins. Do not pin through the actual silhouette, as the pins might leave holes or cause distortion. Remove the tape when the pinning is complete.

Quilt your piece by hand, machine, or a combination of both. Machine quilt straight seams in-the-ditch with compatible thread. Hand quilt around printed motifs with high-contrast quilting, embroidery, or metallic thread. *Do not outline the silhouette or stitch the silhouette down through the batting, as doing so will cause distortion.*

When the quilting is complete, measure the piece carefully on all four edges and through the middle both ways. You can usually eliminate rippling or differences in measurement by blocking the quilt. Lay a large white towel on a flat surface, lay the quilt on top, and mist it lightly with water from a spray bottle. Pat the quilt into place and let it dry completely. Occasionally, you may need to trim a piece to square it. Finally, hand baste between the seam allowance and the outside edge so that they don't slip when you apply the binding.

FRENCH BINDING

French binding is a double-layered binding that is easy to apply, durable, and neat in appearance. It adds a polished, professional finish to the fabric silhouette—especially important for a small quilt that will be hung on the wall and viewed as art. I carry the finish one step further by machine mitering the corners. This method eliminates the step of having to go back and whipstitch the corner folds by hand. It looks complicated, but the more corners you sew, the more proficient you will become.

1. Cut 4 binding strips, each 3″ wide and 3″ longer than the corresponding edge of the quilt. Binding strips may be cut on the crosswise or lengthwise grain of the fabric. Fold each binding strip in half lengthwise, right side out, and press to set the crease.

2. Use a sharp graphite pencil to mark a dot ¼″ in from the edge at each corner of the quilt top. Center a binding strip on one edge of the quilt top, raw edges matching. Let the ends extend evenly at each end. Stitch from dot to dot, using a ¼″ seam allowance and backtacking at the beginning and end. Be sure to start and stop *exactly* on the dots.

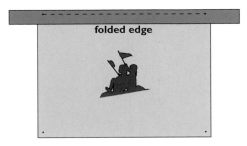

Stitch the first binding strip.

3. Remove the quilt from the machine. Turn the quilt so that the binding is at the top and the excess binding lays flat

at the right edge. Make sure that the corner dot (A) is clearly marked. Measure from A to the folded edge of the binding and mark Dot B. Measure the exact same distance from A to the right, even with the stitching line, and mark Dot C. Measure from B to the right on the folded edge to mark Dot D. Use a small ruler and a pencil to draw a line from A to D and another line from B to C. The lines intersect at Dot E.

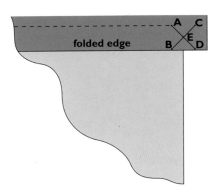

Mark the binding.

4. Fold the marked end of the binding up at a 45° angle. Center the second binding strip along the right edge of the quilt top, raw edges matching. Let the ends extend evenly at each end and overlap the 45° fold at the top.

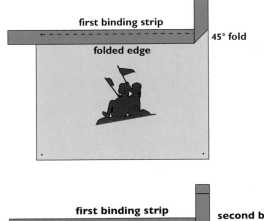

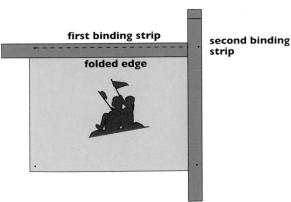

Place the second binding strip.

5. Use your nondominant hand to grasp the two binding strips at the corner dot. Push the quilt and seam allowances out of the way and lay the binding ends flat, with the marked binding strip on top. Insert a pin at A through both layers, being careful not to catch or pin into the quilt. Insert two more pins to keep the edges of the binding even.

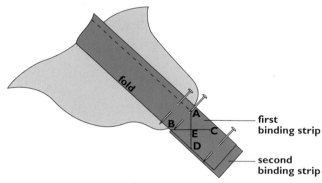

Pin the ends together.

6. Set the machine for a very short stitch length. Backtacking at the beginning and end, stitch from A to E, pivot, and stitch from E to B. Trim close to the stitching and cut off the tip.

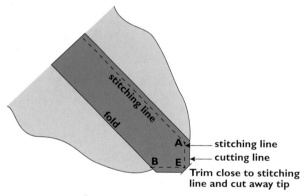

Stitch and trim.

7. Turn and pull out the seam allowance on the second binding strip. Realign the strip on the quilt top, raw edges matching. Stitch from corner dot to corner dot, backstitching at each end, as before. Repeat Steps 2–7 to miter the next corner of the binding. Repeat until all four corners are mitered.

8. Trim off the excess backing and batting ½″ from the stitching line. Center the hanging sleeve (see Hanging Sleeve, right) on the top back edge of the quilt, raw edges matching, and stitch over the previous stitching to attach it. Fold the binding to the back of the quilt, using a point turner or chopstick to turn and push out the corners. Press well. Blindstitch on the back side,

concealing all raw edges. Press the hanging sleeve flat and blindstitch the creased edge to the backing.

Hanging Sleeve

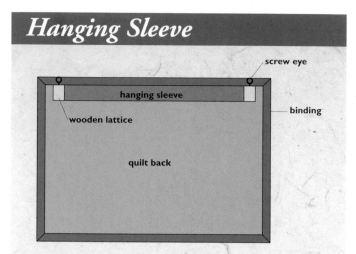

Make the sleeve: Use fabric that matches or coordinates with the quilt back. Measure the top edge of the quilted piece and subtract 2″. Cut a piece of fabric this length × 5½″. Press each 5½″ edge ¼″ to the wrong side and machine stitch. Fold the sleeve in half lengthwise, right side out, and press. This makes a sleeve that is 2½″ wide. Please note that some quilt shows require a 4″ sleeve, so if you plan to show your quilt, you will need to cut your sleeve fabric 8½″ wide. Attach the sleeve to the quilt back (see French Binding, Step 8).

Add the wood strip: Use 1½″ × ¼″ wood lattice. Cut the lattice 2″ longer than the hanging sleeve. Sand it, seal it with sanding sealant, and let it dry. Install a screw eye in the top edge at one end. Slide the lattice through the sleeve and attach the second screw eye. Hang the screw eyes on small nails with heads.

Wen Ling, 10¼″ diameter. Another way to show off your quilted silhouette art is with a very simple picture frame, preferably black and without glass. Choose a frame during the design stage so that you can be sure the background fabric is large enough to fill it. Create the silhouette as usual, but omit the framing and accent strips if they would clutter the design. Have your work professionally framed or consult a framing guide to do it yourself.

Gallery

Original photo

A sparkly red, white, and blue balloon cut from Fourth of July fabric welcomes home our Wen Ling.

Welcome Home, 14″ × 18″

Born at the Right Time, 16¼″ × 20¼″

Original photo

A mother welcomes her firstborn child halfway around the world. They are surrounded by two beautiful Asian prints in green and cream.

Original photos

Barbershop Harmony, 15½″ × 15″

A medley of musical fabrics sets off the members of the Gold Coast Chorus of Coos Bay, Oregon. The technique of cutting the outline of the form away and letting the background show through creates a silhouette from a very poor photo and a grainy newspaper clipping.

Original photos

Blurry pictures downloaded from the Internet blend together to represent the Bridge Town Sound barbershop chorus of Portland, Oregon. Shiny purple vests pop out from the musical score background.

Bridge Town Sound, 25¼″ × 24¾″

Original photo

Sky and water fabrics create a mesmerizing background for this water-gazing pair. Black lines drawn freehand enhance the silhouetted beach grasses. Iron-on bias tape was fused in place and topstitched with a double sewing machine needle to create the black accent strip.

Sisters, 18³/₄″ × 25¹/₂″

A Day at the Zoo, 16³/₄″ × 24¹/₂″

Original photo

The small boy in the silhouette is surrounded by Laurel Burch's exotic animal prints. The black framing fabric relates to the black background in the prints.

This Many, 17¹/₄″ × 21″

The little boy from *A Day at the Zoo* makes a second appearance at the beach. It's his birthday, and he's this many! Cloud and water fabrics surround his perch on a rocky shore.

April Showers, 15$\frac{1}{2}$″ × 18$\frac{3}{4}$″

May Flowers, 15$\frac{1}{2}$″ × 18$\frac{3}{4}$″

Original photo

April showers bring May flowers. The silhouettes in this double wall hanging tell a simple story. A watering can, a May basket, and lots of flowers—it's spring!

Original photo

Our little girl is back, featured on a hand-quilted soft blue floral background set in a black oval frame.

May Day, 10$\frac{1}{2}$″ × 13$\frac{1}{2}$″ oval

A Little Help From a Friend, 16″ × 19¼″

Original photo

A few artfully cut slivers turn a difficult composition into a charming vignette. Even the shaggy dog is recognizable. Black fabric photo corners set off the dark print chosen for the inner oval frame. The blues in the framing and background fabrics relate to one another without matching exactly.

It's the Fourth of July

It's the Fourth of July, 17″ × 17″

Original photo

A fantastic glittery fireworks fabric frames two young flag wavers. The marbled print background adds intense, swirling movement to this dazzling Fourth of July display. The bright red accent fabric is repeated in the binding.

Fabric and Supplies

Good-quality, high-thread-count black solid:

6″ × 7½″ piece for silhouettes

4″ × 10¼″ piece for curb

10½″ × 10½″ red, white, and blue marbled fabric for background

¼ yard dark blue fireworks print for framing

⅜ yard red print for accent and binding

Scrap of patriotic print with 2 American flags

5½″ × 15″ fabric for hanging sleeve

18″ × 18″ backing

18½″ × 18½″ low-loft batting

Black, dark navy, and off-white cotton sewing thread

Off-white cotton quilting thread

Transparent nylon thread

White chalk pencil

Star-shaped cookie cutters

See pages 5, 16, and 21 for additional supplies.

Instructions

For additional information, refer to the technique instructions as noted.

1. Photocopy the modified tracing (page 32). Trace the design onto tracing paper with a sharp pencil to make the pattern. (*The Snapshot Silhouette, page 5*)

> **TIP** *To substitute your own photo, enlarge the figure area to about 6″ × 7½″ and create your own modified tracing.*

Photocopy

2. Iron the paper-backed fusible web to the wrong side of the black fabric pieces and the scrap with the printed flags. (*Applying the Fusible Web, page 17*)

3. Transfer the girls' silhouette to the paper side of the 6″ × 7½″ black piece, using graphite paper and a stylus. Transfer the curb outline to the 4″ × 10¼″ piece. (*Marking the Design, page 17*)

4. Cut out the girls' silhouettes, the curb, and 2 printed flags using small scissors. Use an X-Acto knife and mat to cut out spaces. Cut 2 narrow strips from the leftover bonded black fabric for the flagstaffs. (*Cutting the Silhouette, page 18*)

5. Press the background fabric. Peel the paper backing from the curb piece. Place the curb piece on the background at the lower left corner, aligning the side and bottom edges, and fuse in place. Add the girl silhouettes, flagstaffs, and flags to the composition and fuse them in place. (*Creating the Layout, page 18*)

6. Stitch down the black pieces with black cotton sewing thread. Stitch down the flags with transparent nylon thread. (*Stitching, page 19*)

7. Outline the flags with a black fine-tip permanent pen. Draw in wisps of hair. Sign and date your art. (*Line Work, page 20*)

8. Cut two 3½″ × 42″ strips from the framing fabric. Cut two 1½″ × 42″ strips from the accent/binding fabric. Sew an accent strip to each framing strip. Cut into four 3½″ × 20″ strips. Join the strips to the background, mitering the corners. (*The Fabric Frame, page 21; Accent Strips, page 22*)

9. Layer and pin baste the quilt. Machine quilt the background with off-white cotton sewing thread, following the printed design. Stitch the mitered seams in-the-ditch with dark navy cotton sewing thread. Place a few star-shaped cookie cutters on the quilt and trace the outlines with a white chalk pencil. Hand quilt the star outlines with off-white cotton quilting thread. (*Layering and Quilting, page 22*)

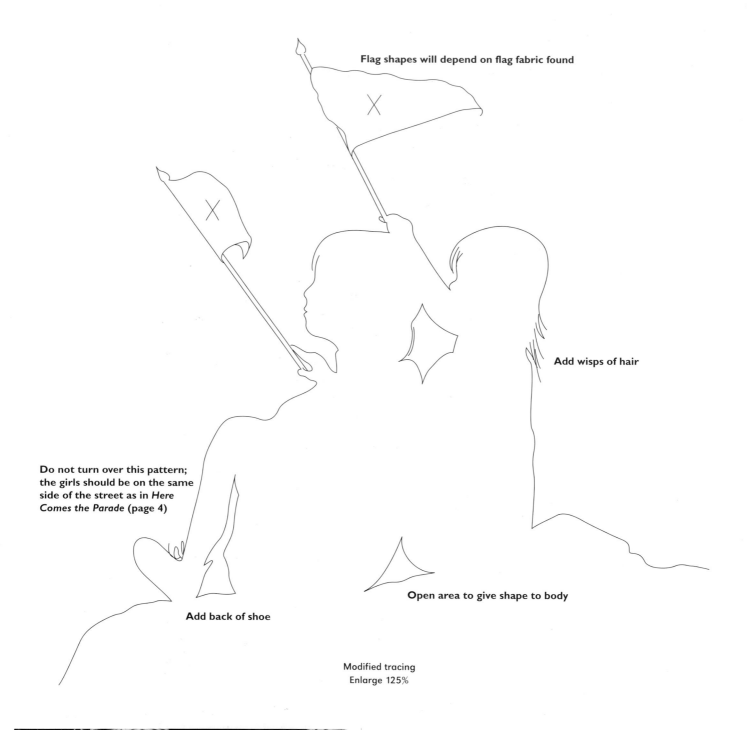

Flag shapes will depend on flag fabric found

Add wisps of hair

Do not turn over this pattern; the girls should be on the same side of the street as in *Here Comes the Parade* **(page 4)**

Open area to give shape to body

Add back of shoe

Modified tracing
Enlarge 125%

Quilted stars from cookie cutters!

10. Cut two 3″ × 42″ strips from the remaining accent/binding fabric and prepare binding strips. Add a hanging sleeve and French binding with mitered corners to finish the quilt. *(Hanging Sleeve, page 24; French Binding, page 23)*

Birthday Party Fun

Birthday Party Fun, 15½″ × 25″

Bright batik balloons float up off the background, adding buoyant energy to a vertical design. Whenever an element extends beyond the expected boundaries, visual excitement results. A birthday girl on a brand-new tricycle provides the necessary counterbalance and reminds us what this party is all about.

Original photo

FABRIC AND SUPPLIES

9″ × 11″ piece of good-quality, high-thread-count black solid for silhouette

11″ × 19½″ piece of light blue print for background

¼ yard blue flowered print for accent

¾ yard black print for framing and binding

Scraps of 5 assorted bright batiks for balloons

5½″ × 13½″ fabric for hanging sleeve

16½″ × 26″ backing

17″ × 26½″ low-loft batting

Black cotton sewing thread, plus colors to match batiks

Metallic thread

Black cotton quilting thread

See pages 5, 16, and 21 for additional supplies.

INSTRUCTIONS

For additional information, refer to the technique instructions as noted.

1. Photocopy the modified tracing, enlarging as indicated. Trace the design onto tracing paper with a sharp pencil to make the pattern. *(The Snapshot Silhouette, page 5)*

> **TIP** *To substitute your own photo, enlarge the figure area to about 6″ × 21″ and create your own modified tracing.*

Photocopy

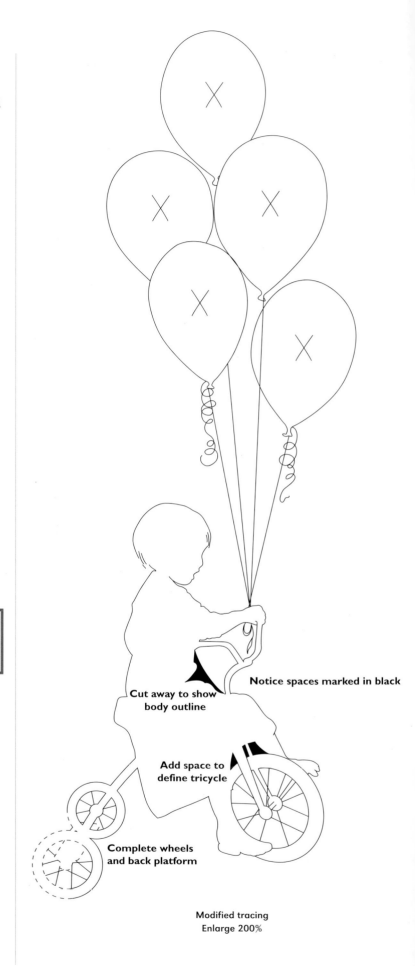

Notice spaces marked in black

Cut away to show body outline

Add space to define tricycle

Complete wheels and back platform

Modified tracing
Enlarge 200%

2. Iron paper-backed fusible web to the wrong side of the black solid fabric and the batik scraps. *(Applying the Fusible Web, page 17)*

3. Transfer the figure and tricycle to the paper side of the black fabric piece, using graphite paper and a stylus. Transfer a balloon outline to each batik piece, placing lighter areas at the top of the balloons for realistic highlights. *(Marking the Design, page 17)*

4. Using small scissors, cut out the figure and tricycle silhouette and each balloon. Use an X-Acto knife and mat to cut spaces. *(Cutting the Silhouette, page 18)*

5. Press the background fabric. Peel the paper backing from the figure and tricycle silhouette. Place the silhouette on the background, using the pattern as a guide, and fuse in place. The balloons will be added in Step 8. *(Creating the Layout, page 18)*

6. Stitch down the silhouette with black cotton sewing thread. *(Stitching, page 19)*

7. Cut one 3½″ × 42″ strip and three 2½″ × 42″ strips from the framing/binding fabric. Cut four 1½″ × 42″ strips from the accent fabric. Sew an accent strip to each framing strip. Trim to make one 3½″ × 19″ strip (for the top edge), one 2½″ × 18½″ strip (for the bottom edge), and two 2½″ × 27½″ strips (for the sides). Join the strips to the background and miter the corners. Note that the top framing strip is wider than the others, to accommodate the balloons, and that the top miters will end at the sides rather than at the corners. *(The Fabric Frame, page 21; Accent Strips, page 22)*

8. Peel the paper backing from the balloons. Arrange the balloons on the quilt top, using the pattern as a guide, and fuse in place. Stitch down the balloons, using matching thread for each one.

9. Draw the balloon strings and tricycle wheel spokes using a black fine-tip permanent pen and a ruler. Draw corkscrews freehand; thicken one edge of each loop to make curling ribbons. Sign and date your work. *(Line Work, page 20)*

10. Layer and pin baste the quilt. Stitch in-the-ditch between the background, accent, and framing fabrics using black cotton sewing thread. Hand quilt the background fabric with metallic thread, following the printed design. Hand quilt corkscrews in the framing with black cotton quilting thread. *(Layering and Quilting, page 22)*

11. Cut three 3″ × 42″ strips from the remaining framing/binding fabric and prepare binding strips. Add a hanging sleeve and French binding with mitered corners to finish the quilt. *(Hanging Sleeve, page 24; French Binding, page 23)*

'Twas the Night Before Christmas

'Twas the Night Before Christmas, 21″ × 18″

Original photo

Batik stars and snowflakes set the mood for a story on Christmas Eve. Who says there isn't a Santa Claus?

The original photo is just a starting point. By changing the background and framing fabrics, any favorite story can be told.

Cinderella, 21″ × 18″, uses a fairy tale print for the background and a sparkling mottled navy for the frame.

FABRIC AND SUPPLIES

12½″ × 15½″ piece of black fabric for silhouette and window frame

8″ × 12″ piece of blue star batik for background

⅞ yard blue snowflake batik for framing and binding

Scrap with a Santa's sleigh motif

4 yards black ¼″ fusible bias tape

5½″ × 19″ fabric for hanging sleeve

20″ × 23″ backing

20½″ × 23½″ low-loft batting

Transparent nylon thread

Black cotton sewing thread

Metallic thread

See pages 5, 16, and 21 for additional supplies.

INSTRUCTIONS

For additional information, refer to the technique instructions as noted.

1. Photocopy the modified tracing (page 38), enlarging as indicated. Trace the design onto tracing paper with a sharp pencil to make the pattern. *(The Snapshot Silhouette, page 5)*

> **TIP** *To substitute your own photo, enlarge the figure area to about 7″ × 9″ and modify as needed.*

Photocopy

2. Press the black fabric and the background fabric. Center the background fabric on the black fabric, right sides up. Machine baste ¼″ from the side and top edges of the background fabric. Leave the bottom edge unstitched.

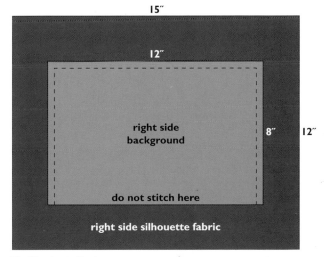

Machine baste 3 edges.

In *Winter Wonderland,* 21″ × 18″, a forest of silver-tipped birches surrounds a snowy winter village.

Grandma's Garden, 21″ × 18″, concentrates color in a bright floral fabric background.

A novelty print inspired the theme and vertical orientation of *Jack and the Beanstalk,* 12½″ × 23″. Can you find Jack?

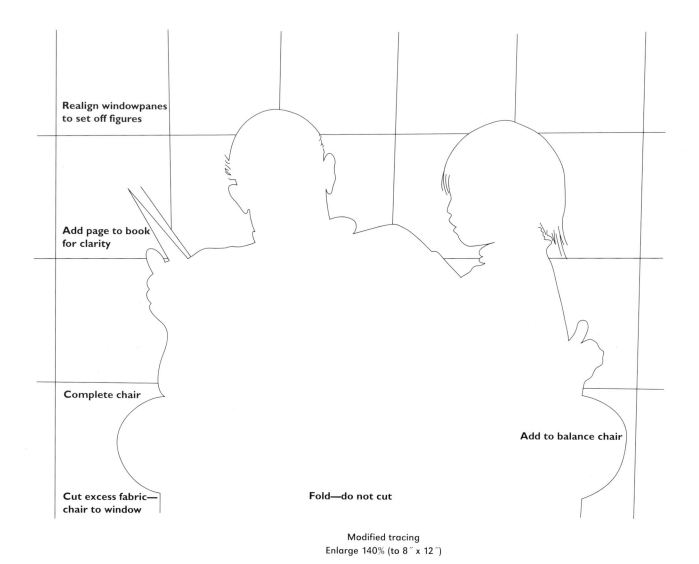

Realign windowpanes
to set off figures

Add page to book
for clarity

Complete chair

Cut excess fabric—
chair to window

Fold—do not cut

Add to balance chair

Modified tracing
Enlarge 140% (to 8″ x 12″)

3. Turn the work facedown. Using a seam ripper, cut a slit *in the black fabric only* ¼″ inside the stitching line. Insert scissors at the slit and carefully cut ¼″ from the stitching line on 3 sides to create a flap.

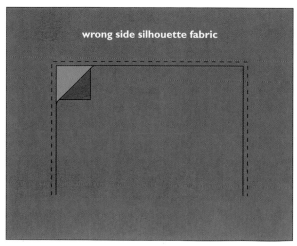

wrong side silhouette fabric

Cut the flap.

4. Turn the work right side up. Pull the flap through the opening at the lower edge of the background. Fold down the flap and press. Iron paper-backed fusible web to the wrong side of the flap. *(Applying the Fusible Web, page 17)*

5. Pin the pattern to the paper backing side of the flap, aligning the bottom edge on the flap fold line as shown. Slip graphite paper in between. Use a stylus to transfer the silhouette design to the paper backing. *(Marking the Design, page 17)*

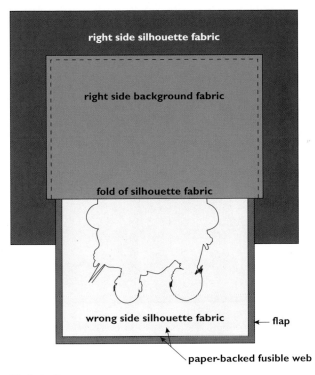

Mark the flap.

6. Cut into the flap along the fold line with large scissors, stopping when you reach the silhouette. Cut out the silhouette with small scissors, keeping it attached to the outer black window frame. *(Cutting the Silhouette, page 18)*

7. Place the pattern right side up on the background fabric. Transfer the windowpane lines to the background, using graphite paper and a stylus.

8. Fuse paper-backed fusible web to the wrong side of the Santa's sleigh motif. Cut out the motif. Place the motif on the background, using the pattern as a guide, and fuse in place. Stitch down using transparent nylon thread. *(Stitching, page 19)*

9. Cut a 2½-yard length of black fusible bias tape. Press the tape in half lengthwise, fusing the edges together. Cut pieces of this narrow strip to match the vertical windowpane lines marked on the background fabric, allowing ¼″ extra at each end to tuck under the silhouette or black frame. Pin or glue the strips to the background, using a ruler to confirm the alignment. Stitch down with black cotton thread. Add horizontal strips in the same way.

> **TIP** *Instead of pinning, use Glue-Baste-It to hold down strips or pieces of fabric for sewing.*

10. Cut pieces from the remaining ¼″-wide bias tape to fit around the edge of the window, to conceal the raw edges. Trim the ends diagonally to "miter" the corners, and allow ¼″ extra to tuck under the chair area of the silhouette. Fuse in place. Stitch down with black thread, using a double sewing machine needle. Pivot at the corners.

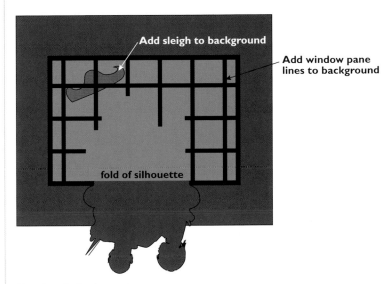

Complete the background.

11. Peel the paper backing from the back of the silhouette. Fold the silhouette up onto the background and press to fuse. Stitch down with black thread.

12. Draw extra pages in the book with a black fine-tip permanent pen. Sign and date your art. *(Line Work, page 20)*

13. Cut four 3″ × 42″ strips from the framing fabric. Subcut into two 3″ × 21½″ strips and two 3″ × 24½″ strips. Join the strips to the background, mitering the corners. *(The Fabric Frame, page 21)*

14. Layer and pin baste the quilt. Quilt in-the-ditch with black thread to outline each windowpane. Quilt in-the-ditch along the inside edge of the framing fabric. Hand quilt scattered snowflakes with metallic thread. *(Layering and Quilting, page 22)*

15. Cut four 3″ × 42″ strips from the remaining framing/binding fabric and prepare binding strips. Add a hanging sleeve and French binding with mitered corners to finish the quilt. *(Hanging Sleeve, page 24; French Binding, page 23)*

Mister Snowman

Mister Snowman, 18¼″ × 23″

Original Photos

Silhouettes don't have to be black. This happy snowman construction crew is bundled up in deep mottled navy fabric. Two snowflake fabrics suggest a swirling snowfall, while metallic silver hand stitching adds to the wintry mix.

FABRIC AND SUPPLIES

9″ × 13″ mottled navy fabric for silhouettes

6″ × 11″ shiny white fabric for snowman

10¼″ × 15″ light blue snowflake print for background

½ yard navy sky print for accent

⅞ yard snowflake print for framing and binding

5½″ × 16¼″ fabric for hanging sleeve

19″ × 24″ backing

19½″ × 24½″ low-loft batting

Dark blue and white cotton sewing thread

Metallic silver embroidery thread

See pages 5, 16, and 21 for additional supplies.

INSTRUCTIONS

For additional information, refer to the technique instructions as noted.

1. Photocopy the modified tracing (page 42), enlarging as indicated. Trace the design onto tracing paper with a sharp pencil to make the pattern. *(The Snapshot Silhouette, page 5)*

> **TIP** *To substitute your own photo or photos, enlarge the figure area to about 7½″ × 12″ and create your own modified tracing.*

Photocopies

2. Iron paper-backed fusible web to the wrong side of the navy and white fabrics. *(Applying the Fusible Web, page 17)*

3. Transfer the children's silhouettes to the paper side of the navy fabric, using graphite paper and a stylus. Transfer the snowman outline to the paper side of the white fabric. Transfer the snowman's hat, scarf, eyes, nose, mouth, and buttons to free areas of the navy piece. *(Marking the Design, page 17)*

4. Cut out the silhouettes, snowman, facial features, and accessories using small scissors. Use an X-Acto knife and mat to cut slivers and slits. *(Cutting the Silhouette, page 18)*

5. Press the background fabric. Peel the paper backing from the silhouettes and the snowman. Place the snowman on the background. Tuck the two taller figures under the snowman at each side, using the pattern as a guide. Fuse in place, leaving the head of the snowman free. Place the smallest figure in front and fuse. Add the facial features and accessories, tucking the hat behind and over the snowman's head, and fuse in place. *(Creating the Layout, page 18)*

6. Stitch down the silhouettes, facial features, and accessories with dark blue thread. Stitch down the snowman with white thread. *(Stitching, page 19)*

7. Sign and date your art with a blue fine-tip permanent pen. *(Line Work, page 20)*

8. Cut four 4″ × 42″ strips from the framing/binding fabric. Cut four 2½″ × 42″ strips of accent fabric. Sew an accent strip to each framing strip. Trim to make two 4″ × 22½″ strips for the top and bottom and two 4″ × 27″ strips for the sides. Join the strips to the background, mitering the corners. *(The Fabric Frame, page 21; Accent Strips, page 22)*

9. Layer and pin baste the quilt. Quilt in-the-ditch between the background and accent fabrics and along the mitered seam using dark blue thread. Hand quilt snowflakes on the background and the frame using metallic silver embroidery thread. Embroider metallic silver French knots across the background. *(Layering and Quilting, page 22)*

10. Cut four 3″ × 42″ strips from the remaining framing/binding fabric and prepare binding strips. Add a hanging sleeve and French binding with mitered corners to finish the quilt. *(Hanging Sleeve, page 24; French Binding, page 23)*

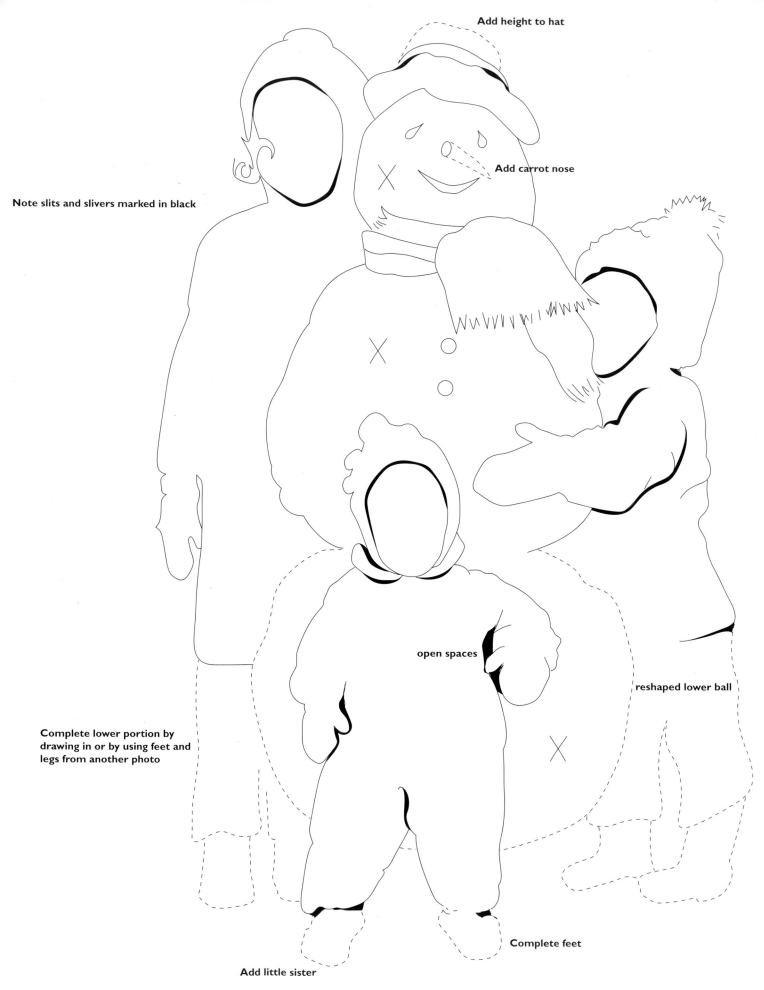

Add height to hat

Add carrot nose

Note slits and slivers marked in black

open spaces

reshaped lower ball

Complete lower portion by
drawing in or by using feet and
legs from another photo

Complete feet

Add little sister

Modified tracing
Enlarge 130%

My Little Cowboys

My Little Cowboys, 16½″ × 20¾″

Original photos

Brown silhouettes mimic the faded, sepia-tone patina that vintage color photos acquire as they age. The look is pure nostalgia. Red plaid and reproduction cowboy prints stir up more memories in this homage to the 1950s Wild West.

FABRIC AND SUPPLIES

7½″ × 8″ dark brown fabric for silhouettes

Two 5½″ × 7½″ pieces of tan print for silhouette backgrounds

11¼″ × 15½″ reproduction cowboy print for quilt background

Scrap of black for photo corners

Scraps of cowboy theme prints for 6 patches

⅜ yard red plaid for framing

⅓ yard brown gingham for binding

5½″ × 14½″ fabric for hanging sleeve

18″ × 22″ backing

18½″ × 22½″ low-loft batting

Brown, tan, black, and red cotton sewing thread

Transparent nylon thread

Off-white quilting thread

See pages 5, 16, and 21 for additional supplies.

INSTRUCTIONS

For additional information, refer to the technique instructions as noted.

1. Photocopy the modified tracings, enlarging as indicated. Trace the designs onto tracing paper with a sharp pencil to make the patterns. *(The Snapshot Silhouette, page 5)*

> **TIP** *To substitute your own photos, enlarge each figure area to about 4½″ × 6½″ and create your own modified tracing.*

Photocopies

2. Iron paper-backed fusible web to the wrong side of the dark brown fabric. Also apply paper-backed fusible web to the scraps with the cowboy patches and to the black scrap. *(Applying the Fusible Web, page 17)*

3. Transfer 2 cowboy silhouettes to the paper side of the dark brown fabric, using graphite paper and a stylus. Transfer 8 photo corners to the paper side of the black fabric scraps. *(Marking the Design, page 17)*

4. Cut out the cowboy silhouettes and the photo corners using small scissors. Use an X-Acto knife and mat to cut slivers and slits. Cut out 6 cowboy patches. *(Cutting the Silhouette, page 18)*

5. Press the silhouette background fabrics. Peel the paper backing from each cowboy silhouette. Place each silhouette on a background and fuse in place. *(Creating the Layout, page 18)*

6. Stitch down the cowboys with brown cotton sewing thread. *(Stitching, page 19)*

7. Press the quilt background fabric. Place the cowboy "photos" on the background, using the pattern as a guide, and pin. Zigzag stitch the edges with tan thread. Add the photo corners to the composition, fuse in place, and stitch with black thread.

8. Outline the outer edge of the zigzag stitches with a brown fine-tip permanent pen. Sign and date your art. *(Line Work, page 20)*

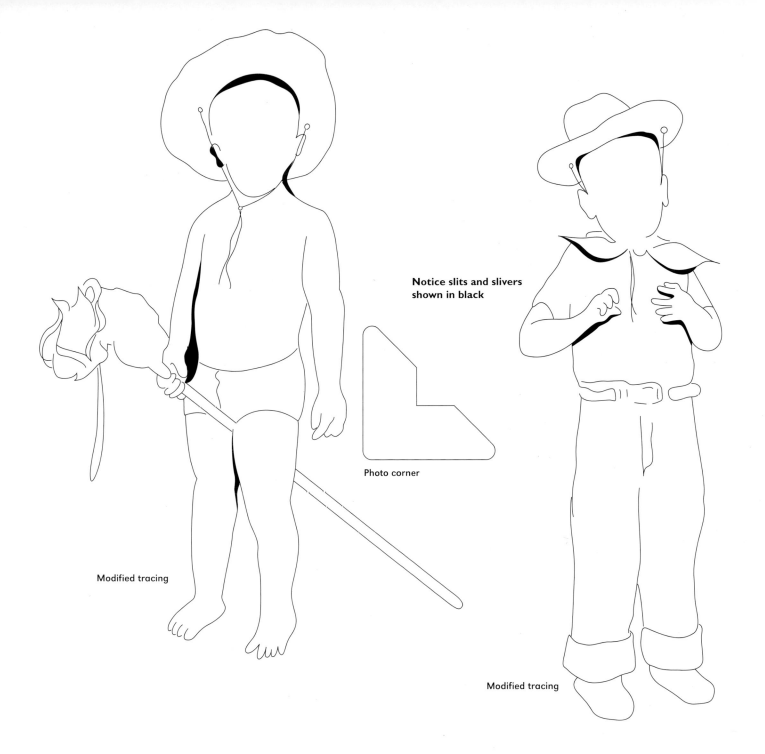

Notice slits and slivers shown in black

Photo corner

Modified tracing

Modified tracing

9. Cut three 2¾″ × 42″ strips from the framing fabric. Trim to make two 2¾″ × 19¼″ strips (top and bottom) and two 2¾″ × 23½″ strips (sides). Join the strips to the background, mitering the corners. *(The Fabric Frame, page 21)*

10. Add the cowboy patches to the composition, allowing them to spill over onto the framing fabric. Fuse in place. Stitch around the edges with transparent nylon thread.

11. Layer and pin baste the quilt. Hand quilt the photo backgrounds and quilt backgrounds with off-white quilting thread, following the designs in the prints. Stitch in-the-ditch between the background and framing pieces and along the miter seamlines with red cotton sewing thread. Machine quilt the framing fabric, following the lines in the plaid. *(Layering and Quilting, page 22)*

12. Cut three 3″ × 42″ strips from the binding fabric and prepare binding strips. Add a hanging sleeve and French binding with mitered corners to finish the quilt. *(Hanging Sleeve, page 24; French Binding, page 23)*

Trick-or-Treat

Trick-or-Treat, 20˝ × 25½˝

Even in their costumes, you know it's *them.* Machine-quilted spiderwebs, grinning jack-o'-lanterns, and a crescent moon keep this little angel and devil company on their annual Halloween escapade.

Original photo

FABRIC AND SUPPLIES

Solid black fabric:

10″ × 13½″ for silhouettes

14″ × 14″ for moon and jack-o'-lanterns

⅛ yard for accent strips

13½″ × 19″ orange spiderweb print for background, plus scraps

Scrap of sheer white fabric for angel's wings

½ yard pumpkin print for framing and binding

5½″ × 18″ fabric for hanging sleeve

24″ × 29½″ backing

24½″ × 30″ low-loft batting

Black cotton sewing thread

Black quilting thread

DecoArt SoSoft Glitters fabric paint, Karat Gold color

See pages 5, 16, and 21 for additional supplies.

INSTRUCTIONS

For additional information, refer to the technique instructions as noted.

1. Photocopy the modified tracing, jack-o'-lanterns, and moon (pages 48 and 49), enlarging as indicated. Trace the designs onto tracing paper with a sharp pencil to make the patterns. *(The Snapshot Silhouette, page 5)*

> **TIP** *To substitute your own photos, enlarge the figure area to about 9½″ × 13″ and create your own modified tracing.*

Photocopy

2. Iron paper-backed fusible web to the wrong side of the black fabric pieces and the sheer white scrap. *(Applying the Fusible Web, page 17)*

3. Transfer the angel and devil silhouettes (omitting the wings) to the paper side of the 10″ × 13½″ black fabric piece, using graphite paper and a stylus. Transfer the jack-o'-lanterns and moon patterns to the 14″ × 14″ black piece. Transfer the wings to the sheer white piece. *(Marking the Design, page 17)*

4. Using small scissors, cut out the angel and devil silhouettes, jack-o'-lanterns, moon, and angel wings. Use an X-Acto knife and mat to cut slivers and slits. *(Cutting the Silhouette, page 18)*

5. Press the background fabric. Peel the paper backing from the angel, devil, and angel wings. Place the silhouettes on the background, using the pattern as a guide. Tuck the wings under the angel silhouette. Fuse in place. *(Creating the Layout, page 18)*

6. Stitch down the silhouettes with black cotton sewing thread. Do not stitch the wings. *(Stitching, page 19)*

7. Cut two 3½″ × 42″ strips from the framing fabric. Subcut to make two 3½″ × 18½″ strips (A), two 3½″ × 13″ strips (B), and four 3½″ × 3½″ squares (C). Cut two 1½″ × 42″ strips from the accent fabric. Subcut to make two 1½″ × 18½″ strips (D), two 1½″ × 20″ strips (E), and four 1½″ × 3½″ strips (F). If you prefer, you can measure the quilt top as you go and cut pieces A through F just before you are ready to sew them.

> **TIP** *If your framing fabric has a directional pattern, first cut 2 A strips on the lengthwise grain. Then cut one 3½″-wide strip from the remaining fabric on the crosswise grain. Subcut into 2 B strips and 4 C squares.*

8. Arrange the background fabric and pieces A through F on a flat surface, referring to the quilt diagram. Join the pieces as shown, pressing toward the accent strips after each addition.

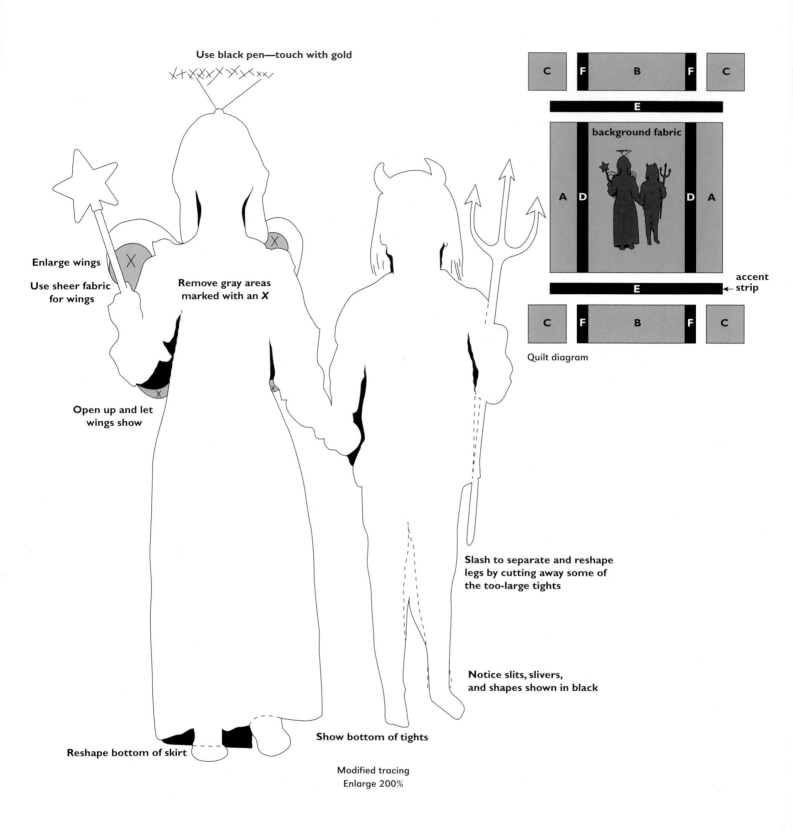

Use black pen—touch with gold

Enlarge wings

Use sheer fabric
for wings

Remove gray areas
marked with an **X**

Open up and let
wings show

Slash to separate and reshape
legs by cutting away some of
the too-large tights

Notice slits, slivers,
and shapes shown in black

Reshape bottom of skirt

Show bottom of tights

Modified tracing
Enlarge 200%

background fabric

Quilt diagram

accent
strip

9. Lay the quilt top right side up. Peel the paper backings from the moon and jack-o'-lanterns. Lay the pieces on the quilt top, referring to the quilt photograph. Cut small pieces of the background print and slip them under the jack-o'-lanterns to fill in the faces. Fuse in place. Stitch down with black cotton thread.

10. Draw a line of *X*s for a halo and a *V*-shaped support above the angel silhouette's head, using a a black fine-tip permanent pen. Brush glitter fabric paint on the halo (but not the support), the edges of the wings, and the edge of the star on wand. Sign and date your work. *(Line Work, page 20)*

11. Layer and pin baste the quilt. Free-motion machine quilt spiderwebs on the background fabric with black cotton sewing thread. Stitch in-the-ditch along both sides of each accent strip. Hand quilt pumpkins in the framing fabric with black quilting thread, following the printed design. *(Layering and Quilting, page 22)*

12. Cut three 3″ × 42″ strips of framing/binding fabric and prepare binding strips. Add a hanging sleeve and French binding with mitered corners to finish the quilt. *(Hanging Sleeve, page 24; French Binding, page 23)*

Modified tracing
Enlarge 250%

First Quilt

First Quilt, 14¼˝ × 14¼˝

Original photo

A patchwork background accentuates this silhouette story: Grandma is helping her young granddaughter tie her first quilt. The sensitive depiction of body language captures both the intent concentration of the child and the intimate bond that develops when one generation teaches another.

FABRIC AND SUPPLIES

½ yard black fabric:

> 10″ × 12″ piece for silhouette

> Reserve remainder for binding

½ yard ¼″ fusible black bias tape

81 assorted 2″ × 2″ squares (dark, medium, and light values)

5½″ × 12″ fabric for a hanging sleeve

16″ × 16″ backing

16½″ × 16½″ low-loft batting

Black cotton sewing thread

Black jeans-weight cotton thread

White chalk pencil

See pages 5, 16, and 21 for additional supplies.

INSTRUCTIONS

For additional information, refer to the technique instructions as noted.

1. Photocopy the modified tracing, enlarging as indicated. Trace the design onto tracing paper with a sharp pencil to make the pattern. *(The Snapshot Silhouette, page 5)*

> **TIP** *To substitute your own photo, enlarge the figure area to about 9″ × 11″ and create your own modified tracing.*

Photocopy

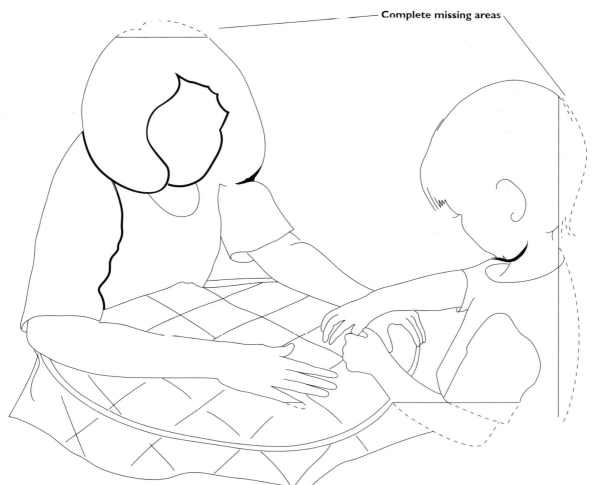

Notice slits and slivers marked in black

Modified tracing
Enlarge 175%

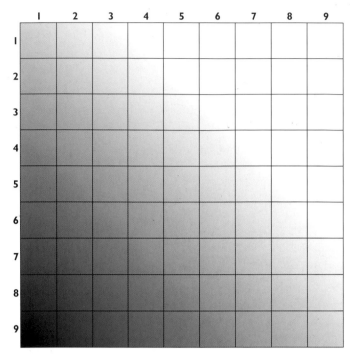

Shading diagram

Patchwork background

2. Iron paper-backed fusible web to the wrong side of the black silhouette fabric. (*Applying the Fusible Web, page 17*)

3. Transfer the silhouette to the paper side of the black fabric piece, using graphite paper and a stylus. (*Marking the Design, page 17*)

4. Cut out the silhouette using small scissors. Use an X-Acto knife and mat to cut slivers and slits. (*Cutting the Silhouette, page 18*)

5. Arrange 81 assorted 2″ × 2″ squares into 9 rows of 9 squares each, so that the values shade from dark at the lower left corner to light at the upper right corner. Sew the squares together in rows. Press. Join the rows. Press.

6. Press the patchwork background from the right side. Place the pattern on top. Slip graphite paper between the pattern and background and trace the round quilt hoop. Remove the pattern and graphite paper.

> **TIP** *Press all the seams in a row in one direction. Alternate the direction from row to row. When you join the rows together, the seamlines will lock into place.*

7. Press the fusible bias tape in half lengthwise, fusing the edges together to make a narrow strip. Pin the strip to the marked hoop line on the patchwork background. Trim off the excess, leaving about ¼″ to tuck under the silhouettes. Stitch down with black cotton thread. (*Stitching, page 19*)

8. Peel the paper backing from the silhouette. Place the silhouette on the background, overlapping the cut ends of the bias tape. Fuse in place, using minimal pressure to prevent the patchwork seamlines from showing through. Stitch down with black thread. (*Creating the Layout, page 18*)

9. Sign and date your art with a black fine-tip permanent pen. (*Line Work, page 20*)

10. Layer and pin baste the quilt. Using a white chalk pencil and a ruler, mark an *X* on each patchwork square or partial square inside and directly below the quilt hoop. Machine quilt the marked lines with large stitches, using black jeans-weight cotton thread. Stitch 3 closely spaced lines to delineate the edge of the quilt. Stitch in-the-ditch to quilt the patchwork background surrounding the silhouetted figures. (*Layering and Quilting, page 22*)

11. Cut four 3″ × 18″ strips from the remaining silhouette/binding fabric and prepare binding strips. Add a hanging sleeve and French binding with mitered corners to finish the quilt (*Hanging Sleeve, page 24; French Binding, page 23*)

End of the Ride

End of the Ride, 24$\frac{1}{2}$″ × 15$\frac{1}{2}$″

Original photos

With the Bandon lighthouse in the background, a tired but jubilant rider ends his 250-mile bike trip down the coast from Portland, Oregon. A watery print that blends sky and sea sets off the silhouettes. Vague geometrics in the frame pick up the city-to-coast theme.

FABRIC AND SUPPLIES

12″ × 17″ black fabric for silhouettes

9″ × 18″ piece of watery blue print for background

1 yard dark blue and purple geometric print for framing and binding (allows 18″ square for bias binding, as shown)

5½″ × 22½″ fabric for hanging sleeve

16½″ × 25½″ backing

17″ × 26″ low-loft batting

Black and blue cotton sewing thread

Navy cotton quilting thread

White chalk pencil

See pages 5, 16, and 21 for additional supplies.

INSTRUCTIONS

For additional information, refer to the technique instructions as noted.

1. Photocopy the modified tracings, enlarging as indicated. Trace the designs onto tracing paper with a sharp pencil to make the patterns. *(The Snapshot Silhouette, page 5)*

> **TIP** *To substitute your own photos, enlarge the figure area to about 9½″ × 11″ and create your own modified tracing.*

Photocopies

2. Iron paper-backed fusible web to the wrong side of the black fabric. *(Applying the Fusible Web, page 17)*

3. Transfer the bicycle and figure silhouette and the lighthouse silhouette to the paper side of the black piece, using graphite paper and a stylus. *(Marking the Design, page 17)*

4. Cut out the silhouettes using small scissors. Use an X-Acto knife and mat to cut slivers and slits. *(Cutting the Silhouette, page 18)*

5. Press the background fabric. Peel the paper backing from the lighthouse silhouette. Place the silhouette on the background, adhesive side down, using the pattern as a guide. Fuse in place. *(Creating the Layout, page 18)*

6. Stitch down the silhouette with black cotton sewing thread. *(Stitching, page 19)*

7. Cut two 3¼″ × 19″ strips and two 3¼ × 23½″ strips from the framing fabric. Sew the shorter strips to the side edges of the background. Press. Sew the longer strips to the top and bottom edges. Press. Place the bicycle and rider silhouette on the background, overlapping the lower framing strip. Fuse in place, as in Step 5. Stitch down the silhouette, as in Step 6.

> **TIP** *If your framing fabric has an obvious directional pattern, cut one set of strips on the lengthwise grain and the other set on the crosswise grain so that the pattern moves horizontally across the quilt.*

8. Align the pattern on the work. Transfer the bicycle spokes to the fabric, using graphite paper and a ruler. Go over the marked lines with a black fine-tip permanent pen. Extend the shoreline on each side of the lighthouse about 1″. Sign and date your art. *(Line Work, page 20)*

9. Layer and pin baste the quilt. Stitch in-the-ditch between the background and the frame, using blue cotton sewing thread. Draw clusters of overlapping circles at the top left and bottom right corners, using a compass and white chalk pencil (or trace around jar lids of various sizes). Hand quilt the circles with navy cotton quilting thread. *(Layering and Quilting, page 22)*

10. Cut two 3″ × 18½″ strips and two 3″ × 27½″ strips on the bias or on the straight grain from the remaining framing/binding fabric. Add a hanging sleeve and French binding with mitered corners to finish the quilt. *(Hanging Sleeve, page 24; French Binding, page 23)*

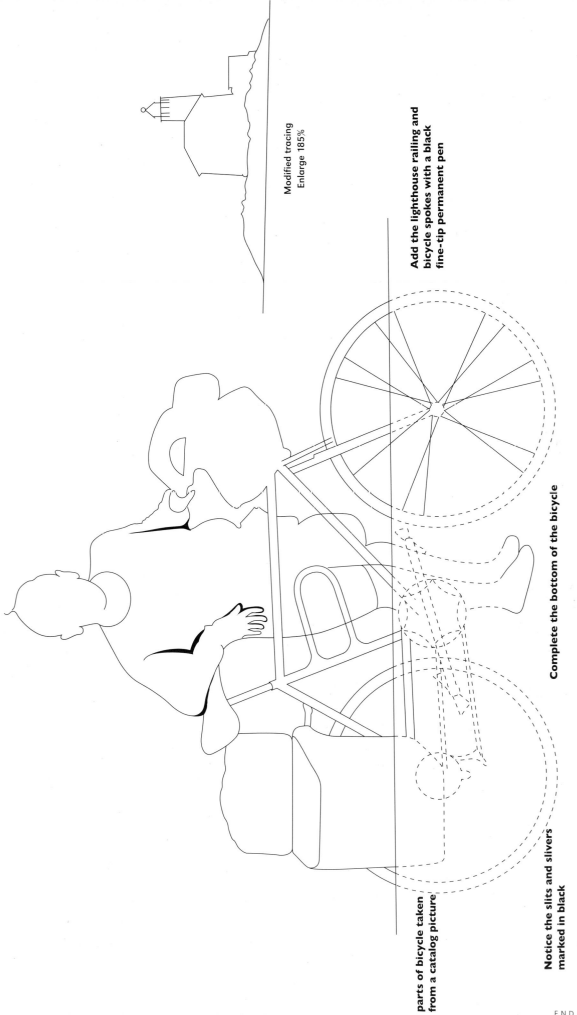

Modified tracing
Enlarge 185%

Add the lighthouse railing and bicycle spokes with a black fine-tip permanent pen

Modified tracing
Enlarge 170%

Complete the bottom of the bicycle

parts of bicycle taken from a catalog picture

Notice the slits and slivers marked in black

Autumn Wedding

Autumn Wedding, 21˝ × 17˝

Original photos

Just a few leaves remain on the branches on a late autumn wedding day. A delicate lace print fabric frames a formal pose, with twiggy branches framing a more informal setting. An heirloom button and batik autumn leaves are just the right touches.

FABRIC AND SUPPLIES

15″ × 22″ black fabric for silhouettes and photo corners

10″ × 13″ shiny white fabric for background

12½″ × 16½″ gray lace print fabric for accent

Scraps of batik fabric in fall colors

½ yard twiggy gray sky fabric for framing

¼ yard gray lace print fabric for binding

5½″ × 19″ fabric for hanging sleeve

18″ × 22″ backing

18½″ × 22½″ low-loft batting

Black, gray, and white cotton sewing thread

Off-white and black cotton quilting thread

White chalk pencil

Shiny white packing twine

Button

See pages 5, 16, and 21 for additional supplies.

INSTRUCTIONS

For additional information, refer to the technique instructions as noted.

1. Photocopy the modified tracings, enlarging as indicated. Trace the designs onto tracing paper with a sharp pencil to make the patterns. *(The Snapshot Silhouette, page 5)*

> **TIP** *To substitute your own photos, enlarge the portrait view to about 9½″ × 12″ and the full-figure view to about 5″× 10″. Create your own modified tracings, using oval photo mats or frames in various sizes to determine the best frame for your portrait..*

Photocopies

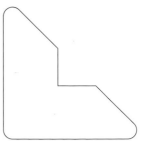

Photo corner

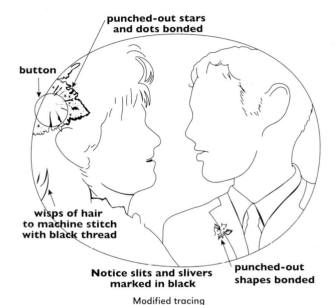

punched-out stars and dots bonded

button

wisps of hair to machine stitch with black thread

Notice slits and slivers marked in black

punched-out shapes bonded

Modified tracing
Enlarge 400%

Punch twice with a star punch to give the effect of a flower

Notice slits, slivers, and spaces marked in black

Modified tracing
Enlarge 220%

Leaves tracing
Enlarge 300%

2. Iron paper-backed fusible web to the wrong side of the black fabric and the batik scraps. *(Applying the Fusible Web, page 17)*

3. Transfer the portrait, full-figure silhouettes, and 4 photo corners to the paper side of the black fabric, using graphite paper and a stylus. Transfer the leaf outlines to the batiks. *(Marking the Design, page 17)*

4. Cut out the silhouettes, photo corners, and leaves using small scissors. Use an X-Acto knife and mat to cut slivers and slits. Use paper punches to make tiny holes in the bride's hair ornament and bouquet. Don't forget to clip your "hanging chads." *(Cutting the Silhouette, page 18)*

5. Press the shiny white fabric. Peel the paper backing from the portrait silhouette. Place the silhouette, adhesive side down, on the shiny white fabric, and fuse it in place. *(Creating the Layout, page 18)*

6. Stitch down the portrait silhouette with black cotton sewing thread. *(Stitching, page 19)*

TIP *To draw a perfect opening, place an oval picture mat on the fabric and trace around it with a white chalk pencil.*

7. Press the gray lace print fabric. Transfer the oval outline to the wrong side of the fabric. Mark a cutting line ¼" inside the oval outline. Cut on the cutting line. Clip into the seam allowance every ½" or less around the entire edge. Fold and press the seam allowance to the wrong side. Place the lace print piece over the portrait. Pin. Stitch close to the folded edge with gray cotton sewing thread.

8. Cut two 2″ × 42″ strips and two 3″ × 42″ strips from the framing fabric. Subcut into 4 strips: 2″ × 20″, 2″ × 23″, 3″ × 23″, and 3″ × 20″. Sew the 2″-wide strips to the left and top edges. Sew the 3″-wide strips to the right and bottom edges. Miter the top left and lower right corners. Miter the two remaining corners so that the seamlines end on the narrower strips. Sew twine along the seamlines with a narrow zigzag stitch and white thread. *(The Fabric Frame, page 21)*

9. Add the photo corners to the quilt top and fuse in place. Place the full-figure silhouette on the right, wider edge, and slip a scrap of white background fabric behind the bouquet. Fuse in place, using a light touch to prevent the seamline from showing through. Arrange the leaves near the top right and lower left corners, using the quilt photo as a guide, and fuse. Stitch down all the pieces with matching thread.

10. Draw in wisps of hair with a black fine-tip permanent pen. Sign and date your art. *(Line Work, page 20)*

11. Layer and pin baste the quilt. Machine quilt uneven vertical lines on the shiny white background to give the appearance of draperies. Stitch in-the-ditch between the lace print fabric and the frame, using compatible thread. Hand quilt hearts with off-white cotton quilting thread, following the designs in the lace print. Hand quilt twigs in the framing fabric with black cotton quilting thread. Sew a button to the headpiece. *(Layering and Quilting, page 22)*

12. Cut two 3″ × 42″ strips of the accent/binding fabric and prepare binding strips. Add a hanging sleeve and French binding with mitered corners to finish the quilt. *(Hanging Sleeve, page 24; French Binding, page 23)*

Reunion

Reunion, 18$\frac{1}{2}$″ × 25$\frac{1}{2}$″

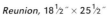

Original photos

Multiple photos were resized and combined to create this joyful composition. Swirling line work adds to the exuberant motion and sense of depth. The Asian bird print chosen for the frame relates to the reunion theme of eight little girls adopted from China.

FABRIC AND SUPPLIES

¾ yard mottled navy fabric:

> 12″ × 12″ piece for silhouettes and kites

> Reserve remainder for accent strips

12″ × 19″ piece of grassy green print with dragonflies for background

½ yard Asian bird print for framing and binding

5½″ × 16½″ fabric for hanging sleeve

19½″ × 26½″ backing

19½″ × 26½″ low-loft batting

Navy and black cotton sewing thread

Variegated green thread

Blue metallic thread

See pages 5, 16, and 21 for additional supplies.

INSTRUCTIONS

For additional information, refer to the technique instructions as noted.

1. Photocopy the modified tracing, enlarging as indicated. Trace the design onto tracing paper with a sharp pencil to make the pattern. *(The Snapshot Silhouette, page 5)*

Photocopies

> **TIP** *To substitute your own photos, size the background figures to about 2″ × 4″ and the foreground figures to about 4″ × 6″, to fill a total figure area of about 8″ × 10″. Create your own modified tracing.*

2. Iron paper-backed fusible web to the wrong side of the navy square. *(Applying the Fusible Web, page 17)*

3. Transfer the girl and kite silhouettes to the paper side of the navy square, using graphite paper and a stylus. Add the kite tail ribbons, but do not add the kite strings at this time. *(Marking the Design, page 17)*

4. Cut out the girl and kite silhouettes using small scissors. Use an X-Acto knife and mat to cut slivers and slits. *(Cutting the Silhouette, page 18)*

5. Press the background fabric. Peel the paper backing from the girl and kite silhouettes. Place them on the background, using the pattern as a guide, and fuse in place. *(Creating the Layout, page 18)*

6. Stitch down the silhouettes using navy cotton sewing thread. *(Stitching, page 19)*

7. Draw kite strings and streamers with a black fine-tip permanent pen. Thicken one edge of the streamer ribbons to create depth. Sign and date your work. *(Line Work, page 20)*

8. Cut four 3½″ × 42″ strips from the framing/binding fabric. Cut four 2″ × 42″ strips from the silhouette/accent fabric. Sew an accent strip to each framing strip. Cut into two 3½″ × 22″ strips and two 3½″ × 29″ strips. Join the strips to the background, mitering the corners. *(The Fabric Frame, page 21; Accent Strips, page 22)*

9. Layer and pin baste the quilt. Machine quilt one edge of assorted grass blades in the background print using variegated green thread. Outline the dragonflies in the print with blue metallic thread. Stitch in-the-ditch between the background and accent fabrics with navy thread. Outline the birds in the framing print with black thread. *(Layering and Quilting, page 22)*

10. Cut three 3″ × 42″ strips from the remaining framing/binding fabric and prepare binding strips. Add a hanging sleeve and French binding with mitered corners to finish the quilt. *(Hanging Sleeve, page 24; French Binding, page 23)*

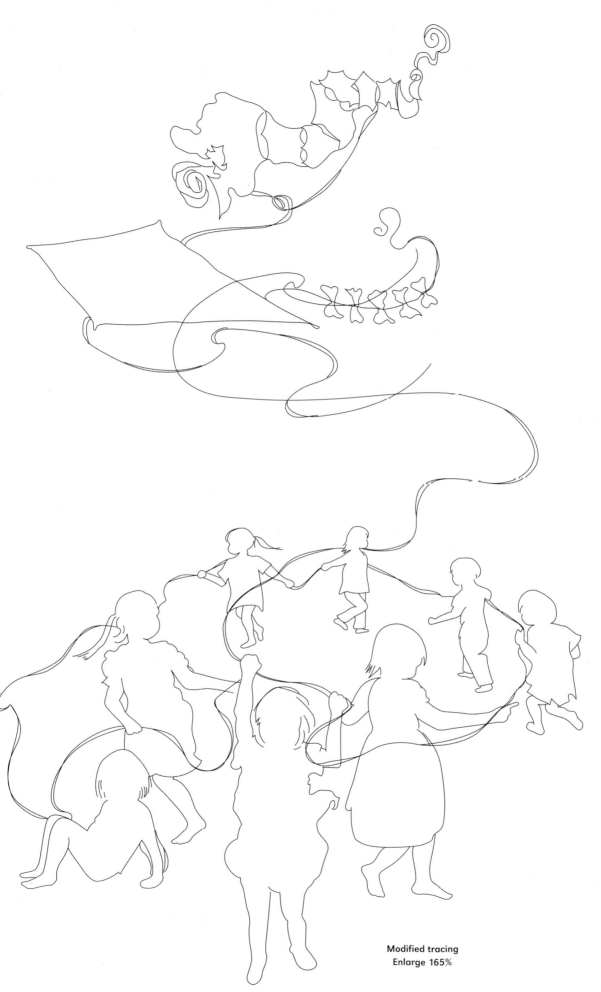

Modified tracing
Enlarge 165%

How Much Fabric?

You don't need a whole lot of fabric to create a Snapshot Silhouette. The fabric requirements listed for each project will help you get started, but eventually you will want to design and make your own projects. Where do you begin?

- **Silhouette.** Use a piece of fabric slightly larger than your photocopy or tracing.

- **Background.** Decide how much space or background you want to leave around the silhouette. Leaving more background space at the top of the silhouette will help ground your subject. Cropping in close to the silhouette draws attention to the subject. Study the examples in this book to see which effects you like. Then place your photocopy on the background fabric and lay picture frames or precut mats around it to help you visualize how different sizes and shapes would look. Be sure to allow room for any other elements you plan to add. Once you determine a size, add a ¼" seam allowance all around. Allow extra yardage for one-way designs that must be placed upright in your project.

- **Frame.** You'll need ¼ to ½ yard of fabric, depending on the size of the background and the width of the framing strip. Use the chart to look up the framing strip length for each edge of the background. You will need four strips total. Use the strip dimensions to calculate the yardage.

- **Accent.** You'll need ⅛ to ¼ yard of fabric. Use the chart to determine the dimensions of each strip. Then calculate the yardage.

- **French binding.** You'll need ¼ to ½ yard of fabric, depending on the size of the quilt. Each strip is cut 3" wide. Use the chart to determine the strip length. You will need four strips total. Use the strip dimensions to calculate the yardage.

FRAMING STRIP DIMENSIONS

Edge of Background Measurement	Framing Strip Lengths if Cut Width is:			
	2½"	3½"	4½"	5½"
8"	14"	16"	18"	20"
9"	15"	17"	19"	21"
10"	16"	18"	20"	22"
11"	17"	19"	21"	23"
12"	18"	20"	22"	24"
14"	20"	22"	24"	26"
16"	22"	24"	26"	28"
18"	24"	26"	28"	30"
20"	26"	28"	30"	32"
30"	36"	38"	40"	42"

ACCENT STRIP DIMENSION

Finished Width	Cut Width	Cut Length
½"	1½"	Same as framing strip
1"	2½"	Same as framing strip
1½"	3½"	Same as framing strip

FRENCH BINDING DIMENSIONS

Edge of Quilt Measurement	Binding Strip Length (Cut Width 3")
10"	13"
11"	14"
12"	15"
14"	17"
16"	19"
18"	21"
20"	23"
30"	33"
32"	35"
34"	37"
36"	39"

EXAMPLE *A piece will have an 8" × 12" background, a 3" frame, a ½" accent, and French binding with machine-mitered corners. The finished dimensions before binding are 14" × 18". Here's what you'll need:*

Frame: Two 3½" × 16" strips and two 3½" × 20" strips, cut on the crosswise grain from ¼ yard of fabric

Accent: Two 1½" × 16" strips and two 1½" × 20" strips, cut on the crosswise grain from ⅛ yard of fabric

Binding: Two 3" × 17" strips and two 3" × 21" strips, cut on the crosswise grain from ¼ yard of fabric

RESOURCES

DecoArt SoSoft Glitters
DecoArt, Inc.
P.O. Box 386
Stanford, KY 40484
800-367-3047
www.decoart.com

Fray Check
Prym-Dritz Corporation
P.O. Box 5028
Spartanburg, SC 29304
www.Dritz.com

Glue-Baste-It
Roxanne Products Company
742 Granite Avenue
Lathrop, CA 95330
800-993-4445
www.thatperfectstitch.com

HeatnBond Lite
HeatnBond
770 Glenn Avenue
Wheeling, IL 60090
847-520-5200
www.thermoweb.com

Pigma Micron pens
Sakura of America
30780 San Clemente
Hayward, CA 94544
www.gellyroll.com

Warm & Natural LowLoft Batting
The Warm Company
954 E. Union Street
Seattle, WA 98122
800-234-WARM
206-320-9276
www.warmcompany.com

X-Acto knives
Bob Corey Associates
Division of BCA Marketing, Inc.
P.O. Box 757
Kresgeville, PA 18333
610-681-7199
www.x-actoblades.com

ABOUT THE AUTHOR

Louise Handley, a fifth-generation Oregonian, was born and educated in Portland. She learned to sew on her mother's old treadle sewing machine. Her paternal grandmother introduced her to quilting and taught her to make strictly utilitarian quilts from used clothing and fabric scraps.

As an adult, Louise pursued decorative painting and became nationally recognized as a self-taught artist and teacher of decorative art. She also refined her quilting skills and began designing and making her own quilts. She has combined her artistic and quilting skills to create many award-winning quilts. One day, while she was placing photos in her family album, the idea of fabric silhouettes came to mind.

The mother of four grown children, Louise is also Grandma to four granddaughters. She lives with her husband of 49 years, Dick, in Bandon, Oregon. When she is not painting or quilting, you will find Louise in her garden, which regularly attracts gardeners, photographers, and tours. *Fabric Silhouettes* is her first book.

INDEX